The Treatment of Normal Weight Bulimia

CLINICAL INSIGHTS

A COMPREHENSIVE
APPROACH TO

The Treatment of Normal Weight Bulimia

Edited by
WALTER H. KAYE, M.D.

Staff Psychiatrist, Laboratory of Psychology and
Psychopathology, National Institute of Mental Health

HARRY E. GWIRTSMAN, M.D.

Medical Staff Fellow, Laboratory of Clinical Science,
National Institute of Mental Health

AMERICAN PSYCHIATRIC PRESS, INC.
Washington, D.C.

Note: The authors have worked to ensure that all information in this book concerning drug dosages, schedules, and routes of administration is accurate at the time of publication and consistent with standards set by the U.S. Food and Drug Administration and the general medical community. As medical research and practice advance, however, therapeutic standards may change. For this reason and because human and mechanical errors sometimes occur, we recommend that readers follow the advice of a physician directly involved in their care or the care of a member of their family.

Library of Congress Cataloging in Publication Data

Main entry under title:

A comprehensive approach to the treatment of normal weight bulimia.

(Clinical insights)
Title on the half-title p.: Treatment of normal weight bulimia.
Includes bibliographies.
1. Bulimarexia—Treatment. I. Kaye, Walter H., 1943-
II. Gwirtsman, Harry E., 1950- . III. Title: Treatment of normal weight bulimia. IV. Series. [DNLM: 1. Appetite Disorders—therapy. WM 175 C737]
RC552.B84C66   1985   616.85'2   85-11180
ISBN 0-88048-077-7 (pbk.)

Contents

Contributors

MICHAEL H. EBERT, M.D.

Professor and Chairman, Department of Psychiatry, Vanderbilt University School of Medicine, Nashville

CAROLE K. EDELSTEIN, M.D.

Assistant Clinical Professor, Department of Psychiatry and Behavioral Sciences; Medical Director, Eating Disorders Clinic, UCLA Neuropsychiatric Institute, Los Angeles

DAVID T. GEORGE, M.D.

Medical Staff Fellow, Section on Experimental Therapeutics, Laboratory of Clinical Science, National Institute of Mental Health, Rockville, Maryland

HARRY E. GWIRTSMAN, M.D.

Medical Staff Fellow, Laboratory of Clinical Science, National Institute of Mental Health, Rockville, Maryland

KATHERINE A. HALMI, M.D.

Associate Professor of Psychiatry, Cornell University Medical College, New York Hospital-Westchester Division, White Plains, New York

JAMES I. HUDSON, M.D.

Assistant Professor of Psychiatry, Department of Psychiatry, Harvard Medical School; Mailman Research Center, McLean Hospital, Belmont, Massachusetts

DAVID C. JIMERSON, M.D.

Chief, Section on Experimental Therapeutics, Laboratory of Clinical Science, National Institute of Mental Health, Rockville, Maryland

JEFFREY M. JONAS, M.D.

Instructor in Psychiatry, Department of Psychiatry, Harvard Medical School; Mailman Research Center, McLean Hospital, Belmont, Massachusetts

WALTER H. KAYE, M.D.

Staff Psychiatrist, Laboratory of Psychology and Psychopathology, National Institute of Mental Health, Rockville, Maryland

JAMES E. MITCHELL, M.D.

Associate Professor of Psychiatry, University of Minnesota Medical School, Minneapolis

HARRISON G. POPE, JR., M.D.

Associate Professor of Psychiatry, Department of Psychiatry, Harvard Medical School; Mailman Research Center, McLean Hospital, Belmont, Massachusetts

RICHARD L. PYLE, M.D.

Assistant Professor of Psychiatry, University of Minnesota Medical School, Minneapolis

SANDRA RAYNES WEISS, B.A.

Psychologist, Section on Experimental Therapeutics, Laboratory of Clinical Science, National Institute of Mental Health, Rockville, Maryland

JOEL YAGER, M.D.

Professor, Department of Psychiatry and Biobehavioral Sciences, UCLA School of Medicine; Director, Eating Disorders Clinic, UCLA Neuropsychiatric Institute, Los Angeles

DEBORAH YURGELUN-TODD, M.S.

Research Assistant, McLean Hospital, Belmont, Massachusetts

Introduction

The eating disorder of bulimia, a current focus of public health concern, is commonly but inaccurately grouped with anorexia nervosa. Anorexia nervosa, first described 300 years ago, has been the subject of an extensive body of descriptive and scientific literature. Descriptions of bulimia in women of normal body weight, however, began to appear in the scientific literature only during the past decade. The interest in bulimia has intensified over this period, and perhaps its incidence has also been on the increase. It is certainly clear from large recent surveys that the prevalence of bulimia in target populations, such as college-age females, is quite high, ranging from three to five percent (1, 2). As such, it represents a health problem of unusual proportions.

What accounts for this surprisingly high incidence? In answering this question, we first must clarify the differences between anorexia nervosa, an illness in which much weight is lost, and bulimia, a disorder of bingeing and purging that occurs typically in women whose weight may remain within normal limits. Bingeing and purging may also occur in anorexia nervosa. The boundaries between these similar disorders are still unclear, and the terminology referring to them is still primitive. This monograph is predominantly focused on understanding and treating the symptom complex of bulimia that occurs in normal weight women.

Speculation currently centers on the influence of Western cultural pressures in the etiology of bulimia. A substantial segment of contemporary culture seems to consider a slim, athletic, prepubertal type of body in women to be most desirable. Women in their late teens and early twenties may be highly susceptible to pressures to conform to this image because this is the period of peak competition for sexual partners. However, bulimia itself has been well known in affluent cultures since Roman times, and descriptions of an entity known as "gluttony" appeared in the English literature of the 19th century. Thus, this disorder may be influenced by more generic cultural pressures.

Becoming a bulimic may also require a biologic vulnerability for affective disorder, substance abuse, or both (3). Investigators (4, 5) have found an increased risk for affective disorder and substance abuse in family members of bulimics. Furthermore, bulimics frequently have neuroendocrine disturbances linked to mood disorders (6) and often can be helped with antidepressant medication (7, 8).

Appetitive behavior and mood regulation appear to share common neuromodulatory systems such as the monoamines and certain peptides. Perhaps bingeing and purging behavior is an attempt to induce in oneself psychopharmacologic alterations that both satisfy hunger and correct dysphoria. Bulimia may be this generation's unique substance abuse invention, coincidently attempting to cope with weight and mood disturbances. In that respect, bulimia might be the 1980s equivalent of drug use in the 1960s; at that time experimentation with drugs served both social and self-medication purposes.

In opening this monograph, Dr. George and associates will discuss the clinical characteristics of bulimia, including prevalence data and demographic information. Included in Chapter One is a review of psychological test studies and family history studies. In Chapter Two, Drs. Kaye and Gwirtsman will point out some of the phenomenological aspects of binge-eating and vomiting while discussing the neurobiological relationships between mood and appetite control. A focus of this discussion is the role of serotonin and norepinephrine, two major neurotransmitters, in the regulation of appetite and neuroendocrine function. In Chapter Three, Dr. Halmi will present a comprehensive review of the medical consequences and complications of binge-eating and vomiting. Her chapter includes a discussion of interactions between bulimia and endocrine dysfunction, such as diabetes.

The remainder of the monograph will deal with issues of treatment and will have direct application to clinicians in the field. Wherever possible, each chapter collates the available data in a given area of treatment. However, in the many instances where there are no controlled studies in the literature, the authors have been asked to propose solutions based upon their extensive clinical experiences. Outpatient treatment has been subdivided into individual and group modalities; Drs. Yager and Edelstein describe individual treatment, and Drs. Pyle and Mitchell cover groups. Inpatient treatment is discussed by Dr. Gwirtsman and his colleagues, and pharmacotherapy is summarized in a paper by Dr. Pope and his co-workers.

The diagnosis and treatment of bulimic disorder are undergoing rapid evolution. Currently, even the terminology is in a state of flux, and the *DSM-IV* may name the illness bulimia nervosa. Because this field is in a state of transition, the information presented here must be regarded as preliminary rather than fully conclusive. However, within those limits, the monograph has been designed to be a practical, cogent, and comprehensive manual that will maximally assist clinicians who deal with bulimic patients.

Walter H. Kaye, M.D.
Harry E. Gwirtsman, M.D.

References

1. Halmi KA, Falk JR, Schwartz E: Binge-eating and vomiting: a survey of a college population. Psychol Med 11:697–706, 1981

2. Cooper PJ, Fairburn CG: Binge-eating and self-induced vomiting in the community: a preliminary study. Br J Psychiatry 142:139–144, 1983

3. Johnson C, Larson R: Bulimia: an analysis of moods and behavior. Psychosom Med 44:341–351, 1982

4. Strober M, Salkin B, Burroughs J, et al: Validity of the bulimia-restricter distinction in anorexia nervosa: parental personality characteristics and family psychiatric morbidity. J Nerv Ment Dis 170:345–351, 1982

5. Hudson JI, Pope HG Jr, Jonas JM, et al: Family history study of anorexia nervosa and bulimia. Br J Psychiatry 142:133–138, 1983

6. Gwirtsman HE, Roy-Byrne P, Yager J, et al: Neuroendocrine abnormalities in bulimia. Am J Psychiatry 140:559–563, 1983

7. Pope HG Jr, Hudson JI, Jonas JM, et al: Bulimia treated with imipramine: a placebo-controlled, double-blind study. Am J Psychiatry 140:554–558, 1983

8. Walsh BT, Stewart JW, Roose SP, et al: Treatment of bulimia with phenelzine. Arch Gen Psychiatry 41:1105–1109, 1984

1

Clinical Characteristics of Normal Weight Bulimia

David T. George, M.D.
Sandra Raynes Weiss, B.A.
David C. Jimerson, M.D.

1

Clinical Characteristics of Normal Weight Bulimia

Bulimic behaviors have been practiced for thousands of years. In ancient Rome, wealthy patricians indulged in orgies that included binge-eating and vomiting. Bulimia as a disorder began to attract attention during the past two decades when several authors described a subgroup of anorexia nervosa patients who vomited to facilitate weight loss after uncontrollable binge-eating (1–3). Subsequent work by Russell (4), Beumont et al. (5), Garfinkel et al. (6), and Casper et al. (7) examined the differences between anorexia nervosa patients who lost weight exclusively by restricting food intake and those who also purged. They found that, compared to restricting anorectics, those who binged and purged tended to be more extroverted, impulsive, sexually experienced, and prone to engage in behaviors such as stealing, drug abuse, and suicide. Beginning in the late 1970s, researchers also began to describe bulimia in normal weight subjects (4).

The apparent recent increase in the prevalence of eating disorders is thought by some to result from the cultural emphasis on the desirability of a slim body and low weight (8, 9). However, while most women in Western culture are exposed to similar pressures to be thin, only a small percentage actually develop eating disorders. The factors that make some individuals vulnerable to societal pressures are poorly understood, but it is hoped that epidemiologic, descriptive, and neurobiologic data may help to clarify the etiology of bulimia and lead to more effective methods of treatment.

DEFINITION

The *DSM-III* criteria for the syndrome of bulimia are listed in Table 1. While these guidelines define the syndromes bulimia and anorexia nervosa as discrete clinical entities, some researchers do not feel they are mutually exclusive (4, 10). This view is supported by the finding that some patients who meet *DSM-III* criteria for bulimia also have a history of anorexia nervosa and share characterological features frequently found in anorexia nervosa patients who binge and purge (11). However, in spite of these similarities, patients who binge-purge and meet *DSM-III* criteria for anorexia nervosa are excluded from the *DSM-III* diagnosis of bulimia. While the *DSM-III* guidelines do not specify a minimal frequency of binge episodes as a requirement for the diagnosis of bulimia, some investigators have used a cut-off of at least weekly binge-vomit episodes when studying the illness (12).

The remaining sections of this chapter will briefly review studies of demographics, clinical traits, psychological test data, and family history in normal weight bulimics. An illustrative case vignette is also presented.

Table 1. *DSM-III* Diagnostic Criteria for Bulimia

A. Recurrent episodes of binge-eating (rapid consumption of a large amount of food in a discrete period of time, usually less than two hours)
B. At least three of the following:
    (1) consumption of high-caloric, easily ingested food during a binge
    (2) inconspicuous eating during a binge
    (3) termination of such eating episodes by abdominal pain, sleep, social interruption, or self-induced vomiting
    (4) repeated attempts to lose weight by severely restrictive diets, self-induced vomiting, or use of cathartics and/or diuretics
    (5) frequent weight fluctuations greater than 10 pounds due to alternating binges and fasts
C. Awareness that the eating pattern is abnormal and fear of not being able to stop eating voluntarily
D. Depressed mood and self-deprecating thoughts following eating binges
E. The bulimic episodes are not due to anorexia nervosa or any known physical disorder

Table 2. Prevalence Data on Normal Weight Bulimia

Investigators	Population surveyed	Diagnostic criteria	Prevalence of bulimia (%)			% of sample who vomited once a week or more	% of sample who abused laxatives, once a week or more
			Female	Male	Overall		
Stangler and Printz (1980)	500 students at college psychiatric clinic	DSM-III	5.3	1.1	3.8	—	—
Halmi et al. (1981)	355 summer liberal art students responding to questionnaire	DSM-III	19	4	1.3	1.7	0.3
Pyle et al. (1983)	1,355 college freshmen responding to questionnaire	DSM-III[a]	4.5	0.4	4.1	0.5	0.3
Johnson et al. (1984)	1,268 female high school students responding to questionnaire	DSM-III[a]	4.9	—	—	2.1	1.7

[a] Frequency of bingeing at least weekly.

PREVALENCE

Epidemiologic studies to estimate the prevalence of bulimia are complicated by the reluctance of many people to admit to binge-eating and vomiting (13, 14). Moreover, criteria for a binge episode are largely impressionistic, complicating attempts to assess binge frequency and severity. Table 2 summarizes data from four studies that have examined the prevalence of bulimia as defined by either *DSM-III* or modified *DSM-III* criteria (the modified criteria specify the frequency of binge-vomit episodes). Stangler and Printz (15) reviewed the psychiatric diagnoses of 500 students at a college psychiatric clinic and reported that 3.8 percent fulfilled criteria for bulimia. In three other studies, questionnaires were used to acquire demographic data. Johnson et al. (16) surveyed 1,268 female high school students using modified criteria of at least weekly binge-eating (not necessarily accompanied by vomiting) and found a prevalence of bulimia of 4.9 percent. Pyle et al. (12), using *DSM-III* criteria, surveyed 1,355 college freshmen and found a similar prevalence of 4.1 percent. These rates were considerably lower than the 13 percent of 355 summer liberal arts students found by Halmi et al. (17) to be bulimic. When the additional criterion of both binge-eating and vomiting at least weekly was applied, Johnson, Pyle, and Halmi found prevalence rates of 0.9, 0.5, and 1.7 percent, respectively. These studies also reported that males constitute 5 to 10 percent of those identified as bulimic.

Pope et al. (18), who administered questionnaires to a broader group of 300 women at a shopping center, found that 10.3 percent of the respondents met *DSM-III* criteria for the diagnosis of bulimia at some time in their lives; of those, 45.2 percent were actively bulimic at the time of the study. Only two of the women with current symptoms of bulimia were over age 30.

In summary, epidemiologic data on the syndrome of bulimia are quite limited at present. Available studies underline the seriousness of the problem but provide limited information because of focus on selected age groups, sampling biases in survey methodology, and probable under-reporting of bulimic symptoms by some respondents. The available data suggest that approximately five percent of college-age women meet *DSM-III* criteria for bulimia (with a frequency of binge-eating of at least once a week). The prevalence of bulimia in men is substantially lower.

DEMOGRAPHIC DATA

In survey data from U.S. and British studies, the usual bulimic patient was a Caucasian female in her early twenties. Little is known about the incidence of bulimia in other cultures. Johnson and colleagues (19) reported that a small percentage of 316 women identified as bulimic were Asian, Hispanic, American Indian, and black. They also reported that a high percentage of bulimics came from upper-class or middle-class families. Because of sampling biases in surveys conducted to date, however, the actual prevalence of bulimia in different ethnic and socio-economic groups is largely unknown.

Table 3 summarizes four recent reports which have described normal weight female subjects with bulimia. Three of the reports are based primarily on university populations. Those by Pyle et al. (20) and Weiss and Ebert (21) were based on outpatient visits, whereas Fairburn and Cooper (14) and Johnson et al. (19) compiled their data from surveys of people who responded to magazine articles. These studies reported that bulimic behavior usually began when the subjects were in their late teens or early twenties, with a range from 11 years of age to 45. Onset appeared to be related to dieting and was frequently associated with feelings of depression, loneliness, boredom, and anger (19, 21). Mean duration of the disorder, as reported at the time of questioning, was approximately five years, supporting the view that bulimia may become a chronic problem. Two-thirds of the women were not married and one-third were still living with their families; most had advanced their education beyond the level of high school. A substantial number of bulimic women were at or slightly above ideal body weight prior to symptom onset. Many managed to lower their weight appreciably by purging.

Table 3. Demographic Data on Normal Weight Bulimia

Investigators	Population surveyed	Diagnostic criteria	Mean age at onset	Mean duration (years)	% Never married	Weight history
Pyle et al. (1981)	34 female outpatients	DSM-III	18 (median) (range 11–45)	4 (median)	64	6 had weighed more than acceptable weight according to Metropolitan Life Insurance Tables; 5 had a history of anorexia.
Fairburn and Cooper (1982)	499 female respondents to questionnaire printed in women's magazine	Russell's criteria	18.4	5.2	—	45% had a history of being over 15% of ideal body weight.
Johnson et al. (1982)	316 females who requested information about bulimia from a university clinic and then returned a questionnaire	DSM-III	18	5.4	70	50% had been overweight in past; 5.2% had a history of anorexia.
Weiss and Ebert (1983)	15 female bulimics and 15 normal controls recruited for research studies	DSM-III	19.7 (range 13–30)	6.4	80	Normal-weight according to the 1959 Metropolitan Life Insurance Tables. None had a history of anorexia or obesity.

CLINICAL CHARACTERISTICS

Typically, the bulimic patient has both a compelling desire to be thin and a preoccupation with food. Weiss and Ebert (21) found that bulimic subjects ate fewer meals and snacks compared to controls (2.9 ± 1.5 versus 4.6 ± 0.8) and restricted their intake to low calorie foods when not binge-eating. Binge periods were irregularly interspersed between periods of fasting or attempts to fast. Surveys indicate that among bulimic patients who seek help, approximately 50 percent binge on a daily basis (19). Mitchell et al. (22), reporting on 40 bulimic patients, found the mean duration of a binge to be 1.18 hours, with a mean consumption of 3,415 calories. While bulimics frequently describe eating cookies, cakes, and other carbohydrates on a binge, Abraham and Beumont (23) analyzed the self-reports of food consumed by 10 patients and found they ate excessive quantities of fat and protein as well. Following food consumption, there is often abdominal discomfort and self-induced vomiting. In addition to vomiting, purging with laxatives, diuretics, and enemas may be used to control weight.

Bulimic patients frequently describe a history of chronic depression compatible with the *DSM-III* diagnosis of dysthymia. The descriptive literature also suggests that bulimia may be related to major affective disorder (24, 25). This argument is supported by the following lines of evidence: 1) A high incidence of affective illness in first-degree relatives of bulimics (25, 26), and 2) improvement of bulimic symptoms with the administration of antidepressants (27–30). From a neuroendocrine perspective, several studies (26, 31) report that 50 to 67 percent of bulimic patients fail to suppress cortisol adequately following administration of dexamethasone. Gwirtsman et al. (31) also found a blunted thyrotropin (TSH) response to thyrotropin-releasing factor (TRH) in eight out of 10 patients with bulimia. The relationship between dexamethasone nonsuppression and blunted TRH responses and depressive symptoms in bulimia needs additional research.

Our clinical experience suggests that normal weight bulimic women demonstrate many of the same impulsive characteristics—for example, suicide attempts, drug abuse, and stealing—

previously described in bulimic patients with anorexia nervosa (6, 7). Weiss and Ebert (21) compared 15 normal weight bulimics with controls and found a significantly higher incidence of suicide attempts, stealing, and drug use in the bulimic sample. Pyle et al. (20) also found high rates of chemical dependency in bulimic subjects and alcoholism in their first-degree relatives.

Thus, there appear to be disturbances in impulse control and affective stability as well as in abnormal eating habits in bulimia. Current research may help clarify the possibility of disturbances in neurotransmitters, such as serotonin or norepinephrine, which may affect these clinical parameters. Alterations in physiological parameters, such as reduced REM latency on sleep EEG, are avenues for additional exploration in bulimia research.

PSYCHOLOGICAL TEST DATA

Numerous studies have employed psychological tests to describe some characteristics of normal weight bulimics.

Nagelberg et al. (32), with the aid of a 21-item screening questionnaire that included a Restraint Scale, divided 244 college women into three groups: subjects who binged (79 percent) or vomited (eight percent), and normal controls (13 percent). Bingers and vomiters scored significantly higher than normals on restraint (a measure of resisting the urge to eat) and compulsive scales. Subjects who vomited scored significantly lower than normals on self-esteem items such as feelings of adequacy and value as a family member.

Norman and Herzog (33) compared restricting anorectics, bulimic anorectics, and normal weight bulimics on the MMPI. The psychopathic deviate scale was the most common peak scale in the normal weight bulimic sample, although the data revealed a similar constellation of personality features in each of the eating disorders. Hatsukami et al. (34) compared personality and behavioral characteristics of bulimic subjects with patients who had drug abuse problems. Patients with drug problems scored significantly higher than bulimics on the MacAndrew Alcoholism Scale and most MMPI scales, but bulimics had MMPI profiles that were indicative of obsessive-compulsive behavior.

Johnson et al. (19) mailed the Hopkins Symptom Checklist to 316 normal weight bulimic women and compared their subtest scores to five groups that had been tested two to six years earlier by other investigators—restricter anorectics, bulimic anorectics, anxiety neurotics, depressive neurotics, and normal controls. The normal weight bulimic group scored significantly lower (less pathology) than the other patient groups on all five symptom dimensions (somatization, obsessive-compulsive, interpersonal sensitivity, depression, and anxiety). However, they scored higher than normal controls on the interpersonal sensitivity scale and depression scales.

Weiss and Ebert (21) also administered the Symptom Checklist–90 to a group of subjects recruited solely for research purposes. They found that their sample of normal weight bulimics scored significantly higher (more pathology) than their normal weight controls on all nine symptom dimensions (somatization, obsessive-compulsive, interpersonal sensitivity, depression, anxiety, anger-hostility, phobic anxiety, paranoid ideation, and psychoticism). The normal weight bulimics also scored significantly lower than controls on five of six self-esteem items on the Piers-Harris Self-Esteem Scale, and significantly higher on three of four obsessive-compulsive items on the Maudsley Obsessive-Compulsive Inventory.

Fairburn and Cooper (14) reported that of all the scales on the General Health Questionnaire, bulimic women scored highest on the anxiety and depression scales.

Johnson and Larson (35) used an electronic pager to signal normal weight bulimics and controls to fill out self-report questionnaires at semi-random intervals during the day. The bulimic women reported significantly greater negative affect than controls on six of eight mood items (sadder, lonelier, weaker, more irritable, more passive, more restrained), exhibited significantly more mood variability, spent greater amounts of time alone, and demonstrated a higher incidence of food-related behavior. As hunger increased during the day, feelings of uncontrollability and inadequacy also increased. Prior to bingeing, bulimics experienced negative mood states—that is, irritability, weakness, constraint. During the binge, the control and adequacy scores of the bulimic group were a full standard deviation below their baseline scores, and there was an increase in guilt, shame, and anger. During the purge there was an increase in alertness and a decrease in anger. After the binge-purge episode all women reported feeling significantly sadder, drowsier, and weaker than usual.

In line with bulimics' preoccupation with food, as described earlier, Hawkins and Clement (36) reported that frequency of binge-eating correlated with the degree of dieting concern in men and women, and in women it also correlated with negative physical self-image.

Herman and Mack (37) speculated that individuals maintaining weight below some biological set-point may be vulnerable to binge-eating. Statistical evidence that some normal weight bulimics may maintain weights lower than their physiological set-points has been published by Weiss and Ebert (21). Pirke et al. (38) provide additional evidence to support such a theory, reporting that some bulimics who were at or near normal weight had elevated levels of free fatty acids and hydroxybutyric acid in their blood. These data are suggestive of intermittent periods of fasting.

The above studies show that normal weight bulimics experience high levels of depression and anxiety, poor self-esteem, mood swings, and feelings of being unable to control their lives. Other manifestations of disturbance are increased rates of suicide attempts, stealing, and substance abuse (19–21).

FAMILY HISTORY

The role of family stress and psychopathology in the evolution of dietary preoccupation and bulimic symptoms, another area of current research interest, is unclear. Pyle et al. (20) found that most of their patients came from stable homes, whereas Nogami and Yabana (39) reported that more than 50 percent of their subjects were the products of broken homes. Garner et al. (11) found that the families of bulimics often had disturbed styles of interaction.

In a nonblind family study, Hudson et al. (25) compared first-degree relatives of schizophrenic and borderline disorder patients with relatives of patients who met *DSM-III* criteria for anorexia nervosa, bulimia, or both. They found that 16 percent of the first-degree relatives of bulimic subjects had a history of major affective disorder, and 55 percent of the bulimic probands had first-degree relatives with a history of major affective disorder. The incidence of depression in first-degree relatives of normal weight bulimic probands was significantly higher than that found for schizophrenic or borderline groups. In contrast, Stern et al. (40) found the lifetime prevalence of major affective disorder in first and second-degree relatives of bulimic probands to be only nine percent, no different from their non-eating-disorder controls matched for sex, race, and age. Stern's results need to be evaluated cautiously, however, because the control group may have contained individuals with affective disorders, thereby confounding the dependent and independent variables. Additional studies are needed to determine whether there is an increased prevalence of major affective disorder in the families of bulimic individuals.

Case Example

Ms. X was a 27-year-old single, white woman employed as a business manager for a retail store. Her weight at evaluation was 117 pounds, with a high weight in the past of 160 pounds and a low weight of 110 pounds. Her height was 5'4". She recounted always having had a "problem" with weight. At age 13 she went on a restrictive diet for three weeks and lost 10 pounds, but subsequently she gained all of the weight back. She had read about purging techniques (for example, vomiting, laxatives) in popular magazines, but her first personal experience with vomiting occurred at age 18. Following a large Mexican meal, she developed an upset stomach and subsequently vomited. Vomiting alleviated her feeling of fullness, decreased her dread of putting on weight, and introduced her to a practice that would allow her to eat as much as she wanted without gaining weight.

At first the practice of purging was uncomfortable, but within several months it became a way of life. Food became her "friend"—a way to quell anger and reduce depression and anxiety. Prior to binge-eating she felt lonely, empty, and depressed, and her thoughts of failure shifted to food. Ambivalence about binge-eating produced a heightened state of anxiety. The decision to binge decreased anxiety.

During the binge she escaped from her world of immediate cares to a dulled, inner-directed state. As the binge progressed she experienced feelings of fullness, fatness, and loss of control. Tension built and then fell precipitously following the purge. What originally had been a "friend" over time became an uncontrollable habit. Consuming a loaf of bread, a half gallon of ice cream, a plate of spaghetti, and a bowl of cereal several times a day was expensive, time-consuming, and isolating, and often took priority over socializing with friends or going to work. In addition, she had difficulty controlling her alcohol intake (she reported frequent periods of drunkenness) and used cocaine regularly.

Ms. X had had a very troubled childhood. On the surface her parents were successful and respected in the community. However, her mother was an alcoholic who had frequent episodes of depression and was often unavailable emotionally for the patient. Her father's behavior was unpredictable, ranging from extreme passivity to displays of frightening rage. The patient was frequently in the middle of family disputes and felt responsible for maintaining peace between her parents. Her parents had high expectations of Ms. X and never seemed satisfied with her accomplishments.

On mental status exam Ms. X was attractive, extroverted, and friendly. She described chronic feelings of depression accompanied by intermittent periods of disrupted sleep, crying spells, and suicidal thoughts. Her affect was bright, and appeared incongruent with her stated depressed mood. She spoke of guilt and shame concerning the binge-eating and vomiting. She had difficulty verbalizing emotion and would often state that everything was "fine."

Physical examination and pertinent laboratory data revealed no physical cause for her vomiting.

DISCUSSION

This case example illustrates a number of the *DSM-III* criteria required to make the diagnosis of bulimia. The patient consumed large quantities of food, became isolated to avoid detection of her behavior, and resorted to vomiting as a way to alleviate abdominal discomfort and to control weight. Over time she experienced wide fluctuations in weight, and the practice of binge-eating and vomiting became uncontrollable. She often experienced dysphoric mood states and felt guilty as a result of her behavior. Other known causes for vomiting, such as increased intracranial pressure or gastrointestinal pathology, were ruled out.

The patient's clinical presentation demonstrated other features often associated with bulimia. She was extroverted but had difficulty expressing emotion and dealing with anger. She was prone to impulsive behavior, as evidenced by a history of alcoholism and drug abuse.

Initially, binge-eating and vomiting made it possible for her to eat as much as she wanted without paying the price of weight gain. By controlling her weight she obtained a much needed sense of accomplishment and was strongly reinforced by society's standards. Anxiety and relief from anxiety characterized the binge-purge cycle. Unfortunately, the advantages gave way to an uncontrollable habit, feelings of guilt, and secretive behavior.

Of special significance to the clinician is the secretive behavior. As mentioned earlier, many bulimic individuals wait several years before seeking help. It is, therefore, important for clinicians to inquire about bulimic symptoms in patients who have a family history of affective disorder or alcoholism, and demonstrate poor impulse control, depression, or inability to express anger effectively.

SUMMARY

In sum, the syndrome of bulimia is an eating disorder characterized by recurrent binge-eating and vomiting. Studies reveal that approximately five percent to 10 percent of college age women and as many as one percent of young men may engage in bulimic behaviors. Symptoms of depression, anxiety, poor self-esteem, mood swings, troubled family relationships, and feelings of helplessness characterize many of these individuals. Bulimics exhibit relatively high rates of suicide attempts, stealing, and substance abuse. Binge-eating and purging serve as mechanisms to regulate body weight and cope with dysphoric emotional states, but ultimately they lead to a troubling sense of guilt and lack of control.

This brief clinical overview of bulimia indicates that many aspects of the syndrome are inadequately understood. Epidemiologic and demographic data currently available reflect limited sample sizes and various recruitment biases. There is little documentation of the natural history of the disorder. The relative roles of psychosocial stressors, personality characteristics, or neurobiologic vulnerability in the pathogenesis of the disorder remain to be clarified. The available clinical and biological data suggest the need for future studies to elucidate further the relationships between bulimia and affective and anxiety disorders.

References

1. Theander S: Anorexia nervosa: a psychiatric investigation of 94 female patients. Acta Psychiatr Scand, suppl 214:1–194, 1970

2. King A: Primary and secondary anorexia nervosa syndromes. Br J Psychiatry 109:470–479, 1963

3. Boskind-Lodahl M: Cinderella's stepsisters: a feminist perspective on anorexia nervosa and bulimia. J Women in Culture and Soc 2:342–356, 1976

4. Russell G: Bulimia nervosa: an ominous variant of anorexia nervosa. Psychol Med 9:429–448, 1979

5. Beumont PJV, George GCW, Smart DE: 'Dieters' and 'vomiters and purgers' in anorexia nervosa. Psychol Med 6:617–622, 1976

6. Garfinkel PE, Moldofsky H, Garner DM: The heterogeneity of anorexia nervosa: bulimia as a distinct subgroup. Arch Gen Psychiatry 37:1036–1040, 1980

7. Casper RC, Eckert ED, Halmi KA, et al: Bulimia: its incidence and clinical importance in patients with anorexia nervosa. Arch Gen Psychiatry 37:1030–1035, 1980

8. Garner DM, Garfinkel PE, Schwartz D, et al: Cultural expectations of thinness in women. Psychol Rep 47:483–491, 1980

9. Schwartz DM, Thompson MG, Johnson CL: Anorexia nervosa and bulimia: the socio-cultural context. International Journal of Eating Disorders 1:20–36, 1981

10. Boskind-Lodahl M, White WC: The definition and treatment of bulimarexia in college women: a pilot study. Journal of the American College Health Association 27:84–86, 1978

11. Garner DM, Garfinkel PE, O'Shaughnessy M: Clinical and psychometric comparison between bulimia in anorexia and bulimia in normal weight women. Report of the Fourth Ross Conference on Medical Research, 1983

12. Pyle RL, Mitchell JE, Eckert ED, et al: The incidence of bulimia in freshman college students. International Journal of Eating Disorders 2:75–85, 1983

13. Herzog DB: Bulimia: the secretive syndrome. Psychosomatics 23:481–483, 1982

14. Fairburn CG, Cooper PJ: Self-induced vomiting and bulimia nervosa: an undetected problem. Br Med J 284:1153–1155, 1982

15. Stangler RS, Printz AM: DSM-III: psychiatric diagnosis in a university population. Am J Psychiatry 137:937–940, 1980

16. Johnson C, Lewis C, Love S, et al: Incidence and correlates of bulimic behavior in a female high school population. Journal of Youth and Adolescence 13:15–26, 1984

17. Halmi KA, Falk JR, Schwartz E: Binge-eating and vomiting: a survey of a college population. Psychol Med 11:697–706, 1981

18. Pope HG Jr, Hudson JI, Yurgelum-Todd D: Anorexia nervosa and bulimia among 300 suburban women shoppers. Am J Psychiatry 141:292–294, 1984

19. Johnson CL, Stuckey MK, Lewis LD, et al: Bulimia: a descriptive survey of 316 cases. International Journal of Eating Disorders 2:3–16, 1982

20. Pyle RL, Mitchell JE, Eckert ED: Bulimia: a report of 34 cases. J Clin Psychiatry 42:60–64, 1981

21. Weiss SR, Ebert MH: Psychological and behavioral characteristics of

normal-weight bulimics and normal-weight controls. Psychosom Med 45:293–303, 1983

22. Mitchell JE, Pyle RL, Eckert ED: Frequency and duration of binge-eating episodes in patients with bulimia. Am J Psychiatry 138:835–836, 1981

23. Abraham SF, Beumont PJV: How patients describe bulimia or binge-eating. Psychol Med 12:625–635, 1982

24. Hudson JI, Pope HG Jr, Jonas JM, et al: Phenomenologic relationship of eating disorders to major affective disorder. Psychiatry Res 9:345–354, 1983

25. Hudson JI, Pope HG Jr, Jonas JM, et al: Family history study of anorexia nervosa and bulimia. Br J Psychiatry 142:133–138, 1983

26. Hudson JI, Laffer PS, Pope HG Jr: Bulimia related to affective disorder by family history and response to dexamethasone suppression test. Am J Psychiatry 139:685–687, 1982

27. Pope HG Jr, Hudson JI: Treatment of bulimia with antidepressants. Psychopharmacology 78:176–179, 1982

28. Pope HG Jr, Hudson JI, Jonas JM, et al: Bulimia treated with imipramine: a placebo-controlled, double-blind study. Am J Psychiatry 140:554–558, 1983

29. Mitchell JE, Groat R: A placebo-controlled, double-blind trial of amitriptyline in bulimia. J Clin Psychopharmacol 4:186–193, 1984

30. Walsh BT, Stewart JW, Wright L, et al: Treatment of bulimia with monoamine oxidase inhibitors. Am J Psychiatry 139:1629–1630, 1982

31. Gwirtsman HE, Roy-Byrne P, Yager J, et al: Neuroendocrine abnormalities in bulimia. Am J Psychiatry 140:559–563 1983

32. Nagelberg DB, Hale SL, Ware SL: The assessment of bulimic symptoms and personality correlates in female college students. J Clin Psychol 40:440–445, 1984

33. Norman DK, Herzog DB: Bulimia, anorexia nervosa, and anorexia nervosa with bulimia: a comparative analysis of MMPI profiles. International Journal of Eating Disorders 2:43–52, 1983

34. Hatsukami D, Owen P, Pyle R, et al: Similarities and differences on the MMPI between women with bulimia and women with alcohol or drug abuse problems. Addict Behav 7:435–439, 1982

35. Johnson C, Larson R: Bulimia: an analysis of moods and behavior. Psychosom Med 44:341–351, 1982

36. Hawkins RC, Clement PF: Development and construct validation of a self-report measure of binge eating tendencies. Addict Behav 5:219–226, 1980

37. Herman CP, Mack D: Restrained and unrestrained eating. J Pers 43:647–660, 1975

38. Pirke KM, Pahl J, Schweiger U: Metabolic and endocrine observations in bulimia nervosa. Abstracts International Conference on Anorexia and Related Disorders. University College, Swansea, Wales, September 1984

39. Nogami Y, Yabana F: On kibarashi-gui (binge-eating). Folia Psychiatr Neurol Jpn 31:159–166, 1977

40. Stern SL, Dixon KN, Nemzer E, et al: Affective disorder in the families of women with normal weight bulimia. Am J Psychiatry 141:1224–1227, 1984

Mood Changes and Patterns of Food Consumption During Bingeing and Purging: Are There Underlying Neurobiologic Relationships?

Walter H. Kaye, M.D.
Harry E. Gwirtsman, M.D.

2

Mood Changes and Patterns of Food Consumption During Bingeing and Purging: Are There Underlying Neurobiologic Relationships?

The distinguishing characteristic of the disorder discussed in this monograph is binge-eating, the consumption of a large quantity of food in a brief period of time. Even though bingeing is the primary characteristic of bulimia, relatively little attention has been focused on this phenomenon. Consequently, while it is generally accepted that bingeing behavior is associated with tension, and perhaps with a disturbance of appetite or weight, investigators do not understand why this is so.

Certain behaviors are associated with bingeing. Subjects report that periods of bingeing may alternate with periods of fasting. Since bingeing or fasting may constitute the only type of eating behavior that subjects engage in, the normal meal patterns are lost. The drive to ingest large quantities of food may be so powerful that others in the household may have to lock the cupboards and refrigerator in order to preserve food for the rest of the family. Substantial sums of money may be spent to buy food. When money is not available, patients may steal food or eat from garbage containers. Social withdrawal is common when bingeing becomes a daily event, and food may become the central focus of the day and the "best friend." Patients may resort to deception and lying in order to continue bingeing. In many ways the tenacity of this behavior resembles substance abuse. What is it about the act of bingeing that serves as such a powerful reinforcement?

It is not understood why bingeing behavior occurs. Does bingeing simply satisfy hunger? If so, why is there a failure to engage the usual satiety mechanisms inherent in regulation of food ingestion? Several studies suggest that bingeing may serve as a form of tension relief (1, 2). The regulatory mechanisms, biologic or otherwise, whereby food intake alters mood are not known.

Bingeing is often followed by purging. Vomiting and laxative use are the most common forms of purging. As with bingeing behavior, little is known about mechanisms that may underly purging behavior. For the purposes of simplification, we will focus on those individuals who binge and then vomit.

Bulimia is often associated with disturbances of mood. Depression frequently occurs (3–5), and there appears to be a genetic vulnerability to mood disorders in patients with eating disorders, since affective disorders frequently occur in their first-degree relatives (6–8). Furthermore, antidepressant medications are often helpful in treatment of depression and in reducing the desire to binge and purge in some patients (see Chapter Seven of this monograph). There are often problems with control of impulsivity (3, 9, 10). Substance abuse is common, and as with affective disorders, substance abuse also occurs in first-degree family members (5).

The above data have been cited by several authors who have hypothesized that bulimia might be a variant of depressive disorders (5). It is not well understood, however, why a range of behavioral disturbances such as depression, anxiety, or substance abuse can create a vulnerability to bingeing and purging behavior. It is even more puzzling how a genetic vulnerability might be expressed in one way in parents, and then be transformed, in the next generation, into the bulimic symptom complex. Perhaps these symptoms have an underlying biological common denominator that might have a differential expression depending on social and experiential factors.

Neuroendocrine disturbances have been found in normal weight bulimia. Disturbed neuroendocrine modulation has been demonstrated in the cortisol (4, 11) and thyroid axis (4, 12). A consistent clinical observation is that women with normal weight bulimia frequently have menstrual abnormalities (2, 4, 9, 12).

Are these disturbances of mood and endocrine function independent of the bingeing behavior in normal weight bulimia, or does some relationship exist between them? Mood, appetite, and some endocrine functions share common brain neurochemistry. This chapter will explore the possibility that a common neurochemical foundation modulates appetite, mood, and certain neuroendocrine systems. A disturbance in one behavioral or neuroendocrine system, or in the neurotransmitters themselves, may spread into multiple systems. We will also address the question of the connection between food intake and stress or tension in bulimia, citing our own study as well as the evidence in the literature. Normally, food intake alters many of the neurochemicals thought to modulate mood. Could extremes of food intake, in biologically vulnerable individuals, through these common neurochemical pathways, be capable of producing significant mood alterations?

BINGEING AND PURGING BEHAVIOR

Time Course and Food Consumption Patterns

The few studies that have analyzed the phenomena of bingeing and purging have used patient self-reports. These studies have found that the number of binges per week, the duration of time spent eating, and the type of food consumed vary greatly among individuals. Mitchell et al. (13) calculated that the range of caloric intake for an average binge-eating episode was 1,200 to 11,500 Kcalories. Contrary to patients' impressions that binges consist of high carbohydrate foods, several reports (2, 13) that reconstructed typical binges from patient histories found that high protein or high fat foods are also consumed.

Because patient self-reports are not always reliable, we carried out a study in which we could observe and document the pattern of caloric intake during bingeing and vomiting, and the mood before and after bingeing and vomiting episodes. Women with bulimia were admitted to an intramural research ward of the National Institute of Mental Health (NIMH). Home conditions were duplicated as closely as possible. Women terminated binge-ing and vomiting cycles when they had achieved a "desired" alteration in mood or appetite. This study verified that patient self-reports were, in general, accurate.

We found that the time course and amount of caloric intake were quite variable from patient to patient (see Figure 1). Each subject who binged and vomited more than once had a fairly stereotypical pattern, in that the amount of caloric intake per binge and the time spent bingeing and vomiting were consistently replicated. Even "small" binges consisted of a relatively large num-ber of calories. During large binges, food intake could reach 166 calories per minute (see Table 1). The percent of caloric intake that was carbohydrate, fat, or protein was quite variable among sub-jects. Our study confirmed the findings that though bulimics state they crave carbohydrates, they will also eat considerable amounts of fat and protein.

Relation to Weight and Mood

Factors responsible for initiating bingeing and purging behavior have been reported as being related to weight control. Abraham and Beumont (2) found that patients reported the onset of such

Table 1. Clinical Characteristics and Data Describing the Bingeing and Vomiting Episodes for 12 Subjects

	Mean	SD	Range Low	High
Age (years)	23.8	3.7	20	31
Height (cm)	163.4	4.5	152	168
Weight (kg)	52.4	7.1	36.5	66.8
Weight (%)	94.6	13.8	62.8	118.0
Total Kcalories consumed	9360	5275	3140	20,650
Carbohydrate (%)	52.0	9.6	37	76
Fat (%)	36.8	8.5	14	46
Protein (%)	11.2	2.2	8	17
Kcalories consumed per minute	113	35	45	166
Time spent in binge (minutes)	29.8	10.2	20	58
Time spent vomiting (minutes)	12.7	8.7	5	29

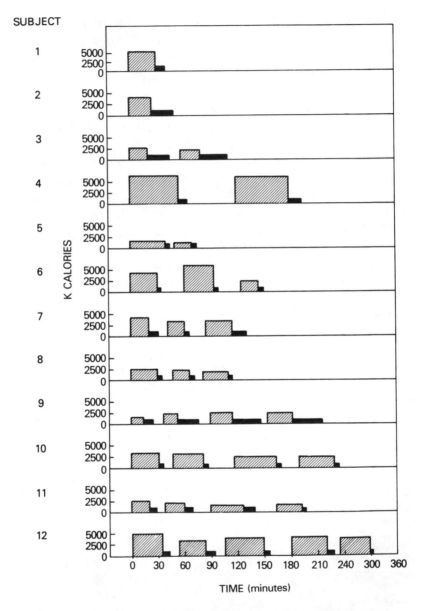

Figure 1. Caloric intake and time course for episodes of bingeing and vomiting for 12 subjects. Shaded area denotes a period of bingeing; the black area denotes a period of vomiting.

behavior after a period of increased concern about body weight and unsuccessful attempts to diet. Chiodo and Latimer (14) reported that 24 of 27 patients learned to vomit as a weight-control method. The possibility that bingeing and purging behavior is an attempt to avoid weight gain is supported by studies that suggest that bulimics might easily become obese (3, 9). Several studies have suggested that a genetic vulnerability to obesity might be present in bulimics if they have relatives that are obese (9, 13). Preliminary work by our group suggests that the caloric intake required to maintain a stable weight in normal weight bulimic women is less than the caloric requirement of normal women matched for age and weight. If such preliminary results can be replicated, altered metabolic efficiency might predispose bulimics to obesity.

Once episodes of bingeing and vomiting begin, apparently they may be precipitated or increased in frequency by stress. Abraham and Beumont (2) listed several stimuli which patients described as being precipitants of bulimic episodes, such as: tension, loneliness, boredom, and thinking about food. Using patient self-reports, Abraham and Beumont found that before a binge, all 32 of the patients in their sample felt anxious and tense. Johnson and Larson (1) reported that immediately preceding a binge there was a negative mood state with increased irritability, greater hunger, and a feeling of being out of control.

The *DSM-III* states that although eating binges may be pleasurable, and although vomiting often reduces post-binge anguish, depressed mood and self-deprecating thoughts still follow eating binges. This is an oversimplification since investigators have found a variety of mood changes during bingeing, after bingeing, and after purging. Abraham and Beumont (2) reported that 34 percent of patients got relief from anxiety during the binge, but for a few patients the relief was temporary and anxious feelings returned as soon as eating stopped; 66 percent reported freedom from anxious feelings after the binge had concluded. Some patients could only achieve relief from anxiety, tension, and negative affects by inducing vomiting. Johnson and Larson (1) reported a worsening of affective state during a binge, with greater guilt, shame, and anger. After the binge/purge episodes had terminated, patients were sadder, drowsier, weaker, and more bored than usual.

In our study, we quantified mood in patients prior to the initial binge, and again after patients voluntarily ceased bingeing and vomiting. Behavior was quantified by two methods: 12 patients self-rated changes in mood on an analog scale (subjective rating). Two psychiatrists objectively rated seven patients by the Brief Psychiatric Rating Scale (BPRS).

On the subjective scale (see Table 2) most patients saw themselves as being more anxious than calm, and more depressed than happy, prior to the initial binge. After patients stopped bingeing and vomiting there was a significant decrease in anxiety lasting two hours, and an increase in satiety lasting for one hour. There was no significant change for depression on any of the other scales.

The objective rating (see Figure 2) demonstrated a similar pattern. There was a significant ($p < .01$) reduction in anxiety for the group as a whole when the baseline rating was compared to the rating completed after the last binge-purge cycle. It is noteworthy that initial anxiety ratings on the BPRS were relatively low. No subjects were in a state of panic. Only two other scales on the 24-item BPRS showed a significant reduction when baseline and post

Table 2. Mean Subjective Mood Scores for 12 Subjects at Baseline and at Intervals After Bingeing and Vomiting[a]

Analog Scale		Baseline	Time After Finishing Binge and Vomit				$F(4,20)$
0mm	100mm	mm	0 Minutes	+20 Minutes	+60 Minutes	+120 Minutes	
Happy	Sad	69 ± 5	59 ± 7	65 ± 7	62 ± 7	59 ± 9	.56
Calm	Anxious	76 ± 6	40 ± 9	48 ± 9	50 ± 8	48 ± 7	6.08*
Hunger	Satiety	39 ± 7	73 ± 9	69 ± 9	66 ± 9	58 ± 10	5.25*
Desire to vomit	No desire to vomit	86 ± 5	68 ± 10	77 ± 8	78 ± 6	78 ± 5	2.04
Confused	Clear	46 ± 10	47 ± 7	45 ± 7	49 ± 7	49 ± 7	.05
Tired	Energetic	42 ± 8	45 ± 8	30 ± 4	31 ± 5	34 ± 5	1.44
Thin	Fat	59 ± 7	65 ± 6	65 ± 6	63 ± 6	65 ± 5	1.62

[a] The changes in subjective rating scores were analyzed by an ANOVA with repeated measures.
* $p = <.05$.

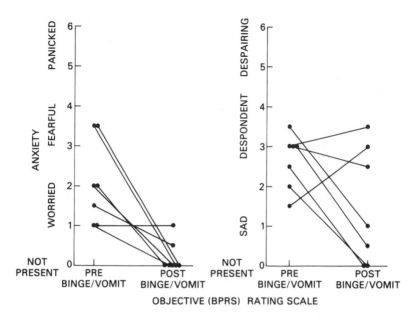

Figure 2. Brief psychiatric rating scale score for baseline and the time of termination of bingeing and vomiting.

bingeing and vomiting scores were compared—the scales for guilt ($p < .05$) and tension ($p < .01$). The pattern for guilt and tension was similar to that for anxiety. Basal scores never reached the most extreme state, and both guilt and tension were decreased in most patients after termination of the last vomit. There was more variation for depression, with some subjects having decreased depression and some increased depression after the last bingeing and vomiting cycle.

It is important to emphasize that a reduction in dysphoria did not always coincide with bulimics' terminating cycles of bingeing and vomiting. The coincidence of an improvement in mood and the stopping of bingeing and vomiting only occurred in five of the 12 subjects. We found that another five subjects had an improvement in mood in the midst of cycles of bingeing and vomiting, yet continued to binge and vomit. For many of these subjects, the improvement in mood continued after they finally decided to stop bingeing and vomiting. In addition, two of the subjects did not improve in mood either during or after bingeing and vomiting. Thus, many bulimics do not stop bingeing and vomiting when they feel better, and a few bulimics continue to binge and vomit without any improvement in mood.

In summary, stress and tension apparently can provoke an episode of bingeing and vomiting. The process of bingeing and vomiting may reduce anxiety and sometimes depression in many but not all bulimics. Bingeing and vomiting also decreased appetite. Thus, bingeing and vomiting may serve to relieve tension and hunger. The mechanisms by which bingeing and vomiting serve to alter mood and hunger remain obscure. Some possible explanations for the link between hunger and mood will be explored in the next section.

THE NEUROCHEMISTRY OF APPETITE CONTROL

Animal studies have discovered much about the mechanisms in the brain that regulate appetite. The neurochemical regulation of appetite is complex, involves a number of neuromodulators, and is not well understood (15, 16). This chapter will focus on only two neurotransmitters, norepinephrine (NE) and serotonin (5–HT). Many other neurotransmitters are thought to modulate appetite but for purposes of simplification will not be reviewed. Animal studies suggests that both NE and 5–HT regulate appetitive behavior in hypothalamic regions. Perhaps more pertinent to the understanding of bulimia, both NE and 5–HT synthesis may be influenced by dietary intake. In this section we will discuss the possibility that bingeing and/or purging behavior produce alterations in neurotransmitter synthesis and thus alter appetite and mood.

In the animal studies, in general, activation of NE pathways in the medial hypothalamus increased feeding. Activation of NE pathways in the lateral hypothalamus or 5–HT in the medial hypothalamus decreased feeding (16). Not only do these neurotransmitters regulate appetite, but they also influence the proportion of ingested carbohydrates or protein. For example, in animals, the administration of drugs that either enhance serotonin's release or suppress its inactivation will increase the proportion of protein to carbohydrate in the total meal (17).

A developing literature suggests that food eaten may itself directly modulate hypothalamic NE and 5–HT metabolism and thus act as a neural signal for food intake. Wurtman has been a principal proponent of the hypothesis that certain food constituents, such as amino acids, may affect the rates at which neurons synthesize neurotransmitters and release them (18). Several mechanisms whereby food might influence neurotransmitter synthesis and release have been suggested. For example, the amount of the amino acid precursors of either 5–HT or NE might directly alter their synthesis (18). A nutrient, such as glucose, might also serve to alter hypothalamic neurotransmitter release (19–21).

If food intake does modulate neurotransmitter synthesis, the process may function to inform the brain about what is eaten. Conceivably, in some biologically vulnerable individuals, food intake produces changes in monoamine metabolism that also influence other regulatory systems, such as mood. The possibility that this occurs in normal weight bulimia is still conjectural, since no data have been published yet on neurotransmitter abnormalities in normal weight bulimia.

Although studies of neurotransmitters in normal weight bulimia have not been reported, differences in concentrations of CSF 5–HIAA, a metabolite of brain serotonin, have been reported in bingeing and nonbingeing patients with anorexia nervosa (22). Bingeing and nonbingeing anorectics have been consistently observed to have differences in mood, characterologic patterns, and appetitive behavior. After probenecid administration (which produces an accumulation of 5–HIAA in CSF), weight-recovered bulimic anorectics have lower concentrations of the serotonin metabolite 5–HIAA than weight-recovered anorectics who did not binge. A decrease in brain serotonin in bulimic anorectics is consistent with what is known about the relation of 5–HT to behavior. Other studies have implicated a disturbance of brain serotonin in dysphoric, impulsive behavior and carbohydrate craving—behaviors typically found in bulimic anorectics. Although anorectic bulimics resemble normal weight bulimics in terms of character structure and mood disturbances, it is not known if there are any similarities in neuromodulator function between these two groups. Studies are currently underway in our laboratory to measure monoamine concentrations in bulimia.

MONOAMINE MODULATION OF MOOD, NEUROENDOCRINE FUNCTION, AND APPETITE

A review of norepinephrine or serotonin modulation of mood or cortisol, thyroid, or gonadotropin function is beyond the scope of this chapter. Interested readers are referred to reviews: NE and 5–HT metabolism have been implicated in the regulation of mood (23–27), and hypothalamic NE and 5–HT pathways are also thought to be among the neurotransmitters modulating cortisol (28), thyroid (29–31), and gonadotropin function (28, 32).

Why do NE and 5–HT systems serve multiple functions in the brain? Morely and Levine (15) have elegantly summarized appetitive behavior and have suggested why the neurochemistry of appetitive behavior might be functionally related to other primitive regulatory systems:

> The integration of the impulses causing appetite regulation takes place mainly in the hypothalamus. The hypothalamus acts as a transducer which integrates the multiple sensory inputs describing the milieu interieur and maintains the nutritional homeostasis of the organism by activating or suppressing the food-seeking behavior of the animal. The hypothalamus carries out its tasks through a complex pattern of monoamines and neuropeptides on a backdrop of hypothalamic interneurons. The same monoamines and neuropeptides that regulate appetite also have a role in other hypothalamic vegetative functions. This overlap in regulatory substances allows a close degree of coordination over related life-sustaining processes. (15, p. 389)

These other life-sustaining processes include multiple neuroendocrine systems, metabolic efficiency, and cardiovascular regulation. Systems such as mood are less well localized in the brain but may have a relationship in terms of similar neurochemistry.

At least three lines of evidence from clinical observations suggest that interactions among feeding behavior, mood regulation, and specific neuroendocrine disturbances are commonplace: 1) Patients with affective disorder frequently have disturbances of appetite and weight. Drugs used to treat depression often alter appetite and weight. Disturbances of adrenocortical and thyroid metabolism frequently are found in mood disorders. 2) People with diseases of cortisol and thyroid metabolism often have disturbances of mood and weight. Animal studies demonstrate that alteration in cortisol and thyroid metabolism have critical influences on mechanisms that regulate appetite and weight. 3) To complete the triad, subjects with eating disorders often have abnormalities of mood and cortisol or thyroid systems.

A Model for Bulimia That Integrates Disturbances in Appetite, Mood, and Neuroendocrine Dysfunction

The biologic link connecting appetite, mood, and certain neuroendocrine functions may be shared neurotransmitter systems. If this is so, then it is likely that NE and 5–HT are among the shared neurotransmitters. (It should be emphasized that this hypothesis is an oversimplification and that there are certainly other relevant neurotransmitter systems.) Could a disturbance in the neurochemical integrity within one behavioral or neuroendocrine system spread, through disruption of normal monoamine functional activity, into other systems dependent on monoamine regulation? We propose a model that integrates the disturbances found in normal weight bulimia in mood, appetite/weight control, and certain neuroendocrine systems (see Figure 3).

This model allows different genetic influences to produce a similar disease process. For example, many normal weight bulimics have relatives with mood disorders and substance abuse. The proband may inherit a vulnerability to mood disorder, which presumably includes a disturbance of some neurochemical system. If this person then happens to discover that bingeing and vomiting produce a short-term relief of dysphoric mood, she might frequently employ such behavior.

Some patients who develop this disorder might not have a

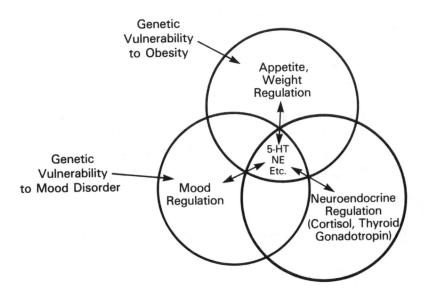

Figure 3. Proposed model for normal weight bulimia syndrome. Each circle indicates an area of pathology thought to occur in this disease. Circles overlap the neurotransmitters norepinephrine (NE) and serotonin (5–HT), suggesting that each of these neurotransmitters influences appetite, mood, and neuroendocrine regulation. Bulimics have a genetic vulnerability to affective (mood) disorder, and perhaps to obesity, suggesting that these vulnerabilities may precipitate the bulimic complex.

family history of mood disorder but might have a genetic vulnerability to obesity. Bingeing and vomiting might begin as a desperate attempt to remain fashionably thin in the face of a biologic tendency to become obese. Bingeing and vomiting might then, over time, produce alterations in monoamine function that spill into mood and neuroendocrine regulation.

Bingeing and vomiting behavior might be similar to substance abuse, with food instead of drugs or alcohol functioning to produce brief improvements in mood or to satiate appetite. The pattern of needing a frequent bulimic "fix, " particularly at stressful times, appears very similar to the dependency found in substance abuse. Could bingeing become self-perpetuating as the victim struggles to avoid withdrawal or rebound effects?

The sequence of cause and effect that occurs between mood, appetite, and neuroendocrine disturbances in normal weight bulimia remains obscure. Bulimia in normal weight women has been recognized as a disease entity only in the very recent past. While much progress has already been made in treating this disorder, little is known about biologic mechanisms that may be contributory. It is important to emphasize that some combination of interrelationships involving both neurochemical disturbances and social pressures may contribute to the initiation and maintenance of the bulimia disease process. The complexity of the systems involved and the limitations of scientific methods leave many questions unanswered. Basic neuroscience research has begun to unravel the brain monoamine and neuropeptide systems that regulate appetite and mood. Greater understanding of such neurochemical systems may have heuristic value in improving treatment for bulimia.

References

1. Johnson C, Larson R: Bulimia: an analysis of moods and behavior. Psychosom Med 44:341–351, 1982

2. Abraham SF, Beumont PJV: How patients describe bulimia or binge eating. Psychol Med 12:625–635, 1982

3. Pyle RL, Mitchell JE, Eckert ED: Bulimia: a report of 34 cases. J Clin Psychiatry 42:60–64, 1981

4. Gwirtsman HE, Roy-Byrne P, Yager J, et al: Neuroendocrine abnormalities in bulimia. Am J Psychiatry 140:559–563, 983

5. Hudson JI, Pope HG Jr, Jonas JM, et al: Phenomenologic relationship of eating disorders to major affective disorder. Psychiatry Res 9:345–354, 1983

6. Gershon ES, Schreiber JL, Hamovit JR, et al: Clinical findings in

patients with anorexia nervosa and affective illness in their relatives. Am J Psychiatry 141:1419–1422, 1984

7. Strober M, Salkin B, Burroughs J, et al: Validity of the bulimia–restricter distinction in anorexia nervosa: parental personality characteristics and family psychiatric morbidity. J Nerv Ment Dis 170:345–351, 1982

8. Hudson JI, Pope HG Jr, Jonas JM, et al: Family history study of anorexia nervosa and bulimia. Br J Psychiatry 142:133–138, 1983

9. Fairburn CG, Cooper PJ: The clinical features of bulimia nervosa. Br J Psychiatry 144:238–246, 1984

10. Weiss SR, Ebert MH: Psychological and behavioral characteristics of normal-weight bulimics and normal-weight controls. Psychosom Med 45:293–303, 1983

11. Hudson JI, Pope HG Jr, Jonas JM, et al: Hypothalamic-pituitary-adrenal-axis hyperactivity in bulimia. Psychiatry Res 8:111-117, 1983.

12. Mitchell JE, Bantle JP: Metabolic and endocrine investigations in women of normal weight with the bulimia syndrome. Biol Psychiatry 18:355–365, 1983

13. Mitchell JE, Pyle RL, Eckert ED: Frequency and duration of binge-eating episodes in patients with bulimia. Am J Psychiatry 138:835–836, 1981

14. Chiodo J, Latimer PR: Vomiting as a learned weight-control technique in bulimia. J Behav Ther Exp Psychiatry 14:131–135, 1983

15. Morley JE, Levine AS: The central control of appetite. Lancet 1:398–401, 1983

16. Leibowitz SF: Neurochemical systems of the hypothalamus: control of feeding and drinking behavior and water-electrolyte excretion, in Behavioral Studies of the Hypothalamus, vol. 3. Edited by Morgane PJ, Panksepp J. New York, Marcel Dekker, 1980

17. Wurtman JJ, Wurtman RJ: Fenfluramine and fluoxetine spare protein consumption while suppressing carbohydrate intake by rats. Science 198:1178–1180, 1977

18. Wurtman RJ: Behavioral effects of nutrients. Lancet 1:1145–1147, 1983

19. Myers RD, McCaleb ML: Feeding: satiety signal from intestine triggers brain's noradrenergic mechanism. Science 209:1035–1037, 1980

20. MacCaleb ML, Myers RD, Singer G, et al: Hypothalamic norepinephrine in the rat during feeding and push-pull perfusion with glucose, 2–DG, or insulin. Am J Physiol 236:312–321, 1979

21. Smythe GA, Grunstein HS, Bradshaw JE, et al: Relationships between brain noradrenergic activity and blood glucose. Nature 308:65–67, 1984

22. Kaye WH, Ebert MH, Gwirtsman HE, et al: Differences in brain serotonergic metabolism between nonbulimic and bulimic patients with anorexia nervosa. Am J Psychiatry 141:1598–1601, 1984

23. Van Praag HM, Central monoamine metabolism in depression, II: catecholamines and related compounds. Psychiatry 21:44–54, 1980

24. Brown GL, Ebert MH, Goyer PF, et al: Aggression, suicide, and serotonin: relationships to CSF amine metabolites. Am J Psychiatry 139:741–746, 1982

25. Traskman L, Asberg M, Bertilsson L, et al: Monoamine metabolites in CSF and suicidal behavior. Arch Gen Psychiatry 38:631–636, 1981

26. Van Praag HM: Depression, suicide, and the metabolism of serotonin in the brain. J Affective Disord 4:275–290, 1982

27. Zis AP, Goodwin FK. The amine hypothesis, in Handbook of Affective Disorders, Edited by Paykel ES. New York, Guilford Press, 1982

28. Weiner RI, Gangong WR: Role of the brain monoamines and histamine in regulation of anterior pituitary secretion. Physiol Rev 58:905–976, 1978

29. Smythe A, Bradshaw JE, Cai WY, et al: Hypothalamic serotonergic stimulation of thyrotropin secretion and related brain-hormone and drug interactions in the rat. Endocrinology 111:1181–1191, 1982

30. Krulich LA, Giachetti A, Marchlewdkako JA, et al: On the role of the central noradrenergic and dopaminergic systems in the regulation of TSH secretion in the rat. Endocrinology 100:496–505, 1977

31. Scapagnini U, Annunziato L, Clementi G, et al: Chronic depletion of brain catecholamines and thyrotropin secretion in the rat. Endocrinology 101:1064–1070, 1977

32. Sawyer CH, Hilliard J, Kanematsu S, et al: Effects of intraventricular infusions of norepinephrine and dopamine on LH release and ovulation in the rabbit. Neuroendocrinology 15:328–337, 1974

3

Medical Aberrations in Bulimia Nervosa

Katherine A. Halmi, M.D.

3

Medical Aberrations in Bulimia Nervosa

Bulimia merely means binge-eating. As indicated in Chapter One, this behavior that has become a common practice among otherwise normal young women and a few young men also occurs in anorexia nervosa patients and in a normal weight condition associated with psychological symptomatology. In the *DSM-III* the latter condition is simply referred to as bulimia and can be diagnosed only if anorexia nervosa is not present. Thus, the *DSM-III* criteria imply that bulimic patients are within a normal weight range. These criteria are merely a description of the process of binge-eating because at the time they were written, there was virtually no information on demographic variables, course of illness, and effective treatment for the disorder.

It is useful to separate people who binge occasionally for a lark from the binge-eaters who have a distinct psychiatric impairment. Russell (1) coined the term bulimia nervosa, conceptualizing the disorder at that time as an "aftermath of the chronic phase of anorexia nervosa." The term bulimia nervosa implies a psychiatric impairment and therefore is a better label for the binge-eating disorder. Additional criteria regarding frequency in binge-eating and maintenance of body weight within 10 percent of a normal weight range are useful for differentiating the disorder from casual behavior and from anorexia nervosa. A proposed revision of *DSM-III* criteria for bulimia or bulimia nervosa is presented in Table 1.

PHYSICAL SIGNS

Distinct physical signs present in bulimia nervosa provide a helpful clue for diagnosis in patients who are reluctant to tell a physician or a therapist about their bingeing and purging behavior. Abrasions and scars on the dorsum of the hands—known as "Russell's sign" because of his initial description (1)—are the result of scraping the hand against teeth while trying to self-induce vomiting.

Erosion of the teeth and poor gum hygiene often provide clues for the diagnosis of bulimia nervosa by the dentist, who frequently is the first to diagnose the condition. Patients with bulimia nervosa can have severe attrition and erosion of the teeth, causing an irritating sensitivity, pathologic pulp exposures, loss of integrity of the dental arches, diminished masticatory ability, and an unaesthetic appearance (2). These changes may result in chronic or permanent disfigurement.

Table 1. Proposed Revision of *DSM-III* Criteria for Bulimia

A. Recurrent episodes of binge-eating (rapid consumption of a large amount of food in a discrete period of time, usually less than two hours).
B. At least three of the following:
    (1) Consumption of a high-caloric, easily ingested food during a binge.
    (2) Inconspicuous eating during a binge.
    (3) Termination of such eating episodes by abdominal pain, sleep, social interruption, or self-induced vomiting.
    (4) Repeated attempts to lose weight by severely restricted diets, self-induced vomiting, or use of cathartics or diuretics.
    (5) Frequent weight fluctuations greater than 10 pounds due to alternating binges and fasts.
C. Awareness that the eating pattern is abnormal and fear of not being able to stop eating voluntarily.
D. Frequency of binge-eating must be an average of at least once per week for a chronicity of three months.
E. Maintenance of body weight within 10 percent of a normal weight range for age, sex, and height.
Type I—for patients who have not had a previous history of anorexia nervosa.
Type II—for patients with a previous history of anorexia nervosa.

Bilateral parotid gland enlargement is another "telltale" mark of bulimia nervosa. Often the parotid gland swelling is intermittent and occurs one to two days after binge-eating episodes. The physiological mechanism of parotid gland enlargement in bulimia nervosa is unknown. Biopsies have show normal glandular tissue (3).

MEDICAL EMERGENCIES

Acute gastric dilatation has usually been described in patients with anorexia nervosa during refeeding (4). The malnourished clinical state of the anorectics has been given as a possible reason for the development of gastric dilatation via a "superior mesentery artery syndrome." Recently, however, gastric dilatation has also been reported in normal weight bulimia nervosa (5). The mechanism for the development of this condition is not known. Severe abdominal pain in a bulimia nervosa patient should alert the physician to a diagnosis of gastric dilatation and the need for nasogastric suction, x-rays, and surgical consultation. Most cases in anorectics have been handled effectively with conservative management, including nasogastric suction and careful monitoring of vital signs. All cases should have a surgical consultation, and some in fact may require surgery. The serious consequence of gastric dilatation is a potentially fatal gastric rupture (6).

Esophageal tears are another potential hazard in bulimia nervosa when patients self-induce vomiting. A complication of shock could result subsequent to the esophageal tear and should be treated by experienced medical and surgical personnel.

Cardiac failure caused by cardiomyopathy from ipecac (emetine) intoxication is a medical emergency that is being reported more frequently and usually results in death (7). Symptoms of precardial pain, dyspnea, and generalized muscle weakness associated with hypotension, tachycardia, and electrocardiogram (EKG) abnormalities of flattening and inversion of T waves in all leads and prolongation of QT intervals should alert one to ipecac intoxication. Other laboratory findings may include elevated serum glutamic-oxalacetic transaminase (SGOT), serum glutamic-pyruvic transaminase (SGPT), creatinine phosphorinase, lactate dehydrogenase (LDH), aldolase, and erythrocyte sedimentation rate. Obviously, a patient in this condition needs to be under a cardiologist's care. An echocardiogram will show a congestive type of cardiomyopathy contraction pattern.

SERUM ELECTROLYTE ABNORMALITIES

Purging behaviors such as self-induced vomiting or abuse of laxatives can lead to the development of metabolic alkalosis or a hypokalemic alkalosis. In one study (8), 49 percent of the bulimia nervosa patients had electrolyte abnormalities, which included elevated serum bicarbonate, hypochloremia, hypokalemia, and in a few cases a low serum bicarbonate, indicating a metabolic acidosis. The latter was particularly true in laxative abusers. It is important to remember that fasting can promote dehydration, which results in volume depletion; that in turn can promote generation of aldosterone, which promotes further potassium excretion from the kidneys. Thus there can be an indirect renal loss of potassium as well as a direct loss through self-induced vomiting. Patients with electrolyte disturbances have physical symptoms of weakness, lethargy, and at times cardiac arrhythmias. There is a danger of cardiac arrest occurring during an arrhythmic episode.

There are most likely multiple mechanisms for cardiac arrhythmias and sudden death in bulimic patients. Some current studies are showing that normal weight bulimics with normal serum electrolytes can have severe cardiac rhythm disturbances (8). These findings lend some support to the postulation that the electrocardiographic abnormalities in the eating disorders may be brought about by stimulations of sympathetic centers within the hypothalamus. These EKG changes are usually irregularities of the T wave, which is flat or inverted, depression of ST segments, and at times a distinct U wave.

Although many clinicians are treating hypokalemia in bulimics with supplemental potassium, this treatment may be more beneficial to the clinicians than to the patients. The best way to treat the hypokalemia is to stop the purging behavior. If the serum potassium falls below 2.5 mmol per liter, the patient should be hospitalized to have serum electrolytes restored to normal range. In a controlled, structured environment this can be done with oral fluids and supplemental potassium. If purging behavior cannot be completely controlled, electrolyte correction may have to be done intravenously. An EKG should be obtained and repeated if abnormalities are present. All serum electrolyte abnormalities are best corrected by stopping the purging behavior. Hypokalemia is the most serious problem because of associated cardiac arrhythmias. Dehydration, metabolic alkalosis, or acidosis can always be corrected with appropriate intravenous fluids, but often oral fluids are sufficient provided that the purging behavior can be controlled in a structured environment.

SERUM ENZYME ABNORMALITIES

In one study serum amylase levels were elevated in 30 of 108 bulimia nervosa patients (8); the frequency of elevated amylase values was significantly higher in patients who reported more frequent binge-eating and in patients reporting more frequent vomiting (8). Checking serum amylase levels may be an effective way to monitor bingeing and vomiting behavior in a bulimia nervosa patient.

It is not unusual for serum enzymes reflecting liver function to be elevated in anorexia nervosa. It is less likely these enzymes are elevated in bulimia nervosa. Serum glutamic-oxalacetic transaminase (SGOT), lactate dehydrogenase (LDH), and alkaline phosphatase are the enzymes most frequently elevated (9). The elevation of these enzymes probably reflects fatty degeneration of the liver.

There is evidence that anorexia nervosa patients, especially those who have been self-inducing vomiting for several years, have osteoporosis (10, 11). In some cases symptoms of pain led to appropriate x-rays, which showed rib fractures, hip fracture, and compression fractures of the vertebrae (10). Since these fractures have been associated mainly with anorectics who engage in self-induced vomiting, it is important to be alert to these problems in bulimics who have been purging for years.

A preliminary report (12) indicated that serum levels of bone isoenzyme of alkaline phosphatase are increased during refeeding of anorectics. In this study the liver alkaline phosphatase isoenzyme serum levels did not change. The periodic episodes of fasting with binge-eating may bring about a disturbed nutrition affecting bone metabolism in bulimia nervosa patients. An increase in alkaline phosphatase could be a sensitive measure for detecting changes in bone metabolism and should be assessed in chronic bulimia nervosa patients.

COMPLICATIONS OF BULIMIA NERVOSA WITH DIABETES MELLITUS

The occurrence of diabetes mellitus with bulimia can present one of the most difficult medical and psychiatric management problems (13, 14). Medical management is impossible until the patient can modify her abnormal eating behavior, and psychiatric therapy is not possible while blood sugar is out of control. A carefully coordinated medical and psychiatric program is necessary to care for these patients, and even then the coordinated program often fails.

ENDOCRINE ABNORMALITIES

Despite abnormal eating patterns, bulimic patients in one study (15) had normal fasting plasma glucose concentrations and a normal glucose tolerance curve.

Contradictory results have been obtained from thyrotropin-releasing hormone (TRH) tests. One study showed a normal thyroid-stimulating hormone (TSH) response to TRH (15), and another showed a blunting of the response in eight of 10 patients (16). Serum thyroxine and T_3 levels are usually within a normal range in bulimic patients. There are some strictly anecdotal stories of a few recalcitrant bulimics responding to supplemental T_3. These patients might have been depressed and therefore responsive to antidepressants, or they might have been chronic recalcitrant depressed bulimics whose response to antidepressant medication is more effective with T_3. Supplemental T_3 medication for bulimics should be considered only in severely recalcitrant patients who can have adequate cardiac monitoring.

Basal levels of growth hormone are normal in bulimia nervosa, but an abnormal increase in serum growth hormone followed TRH administration (15), and growth hormone failed to suppress normally after oral glucose in half of the subjects tested. Abnormal growth hormone responses in bulimics may be related to their eating pattern, or they may represent a nonspecific manifestation of stress or illness.

In one study, 12 of 18 patents had abnormal dexamethasone suppression tests, meaning they had an abnormality of cortisol suppression (16). In another study about one-half of 47 patients with bulimia were nonsuppressors to dexamethasone (17). The physiological meaning of these findings is not clear. Neither study associated the degree of depression or a diagnosis of major depressive disorder with response to dexamethasone in the bulimic patients. The cortisol response to dexamethasone may reflect acute changes in weight from the fasting to bingeing state. Although sporadic menstrual irregularities are reported in bulimia nervosa patients, and on occasion they are the presenting symptom, careful systematic studies of follicle-stimulating hormone (FSH) and luteinizing hormone (LH) secretion have not been conducted in these patients. Only a few preliminary studies are available on the endocrinology of bulimia nervosa. Obviously it is not possible to draw conclusions over hypothalamic-pituitary-target organ abnormalities in this disorder at present.

The death rate in normal weight bulimia nervosa patients is not known. There has been no follow-up of adequate numbers of these patients over a sufficient period of time so that a meaningful death rate can be calculated. Bulimia nervosa patients die of cardiac arrest (which may or may not be associated with serum electrolyte abnormalities), cardiac failure (which may be associated with ipecac intoxication), gastric dilatation, and esophageal tears. Patients who binge and purge and are chronically underweight may incur additional complications from chronic malnourishment.

The initial medical evaluation of a bulimia nervosa patient should include serum electrolytes and enzymes, an EKG, and a dental examination. The frequency in repeating these studies will depend on the severity of the bingeing and purging and on the initial findings. Since elevation of serum amylase is associated with severity of bingeing and purging, it is reasonable to obtain a serum amylase level periodically on these patients.

The medical problems in bulimia nervosa appear to be directly related to the bingeing and purging behavior. Subtle abnormalities in the physiological mechanisms of appetite and satiety are more difficult to assess, as are subtle aberrations in the endorphin system. Investigation of the physiology of bulimia nervosa is relatively recent. Studies of chronic bulimia nervosa patients will add a new dimension that should be helpful in understanding the physiology of this disorder.

References

1. Russell G: Bulimia nervosa: an ominous variant of anorexia nervosa. Psychol Med 9:429–448, 1979

2. Stege P: Anorexia nervosa: review including oral and dental manifestations. J Am Dental Assoc 104:648–652, 1982

3. Hasler JF: Parotic enlargement: a presenting sign of anorexia nervosa. Oral Medicine 6:567–573, 1982

4. Jennings K, Klidjian A: Acute gastric dilatation in anorexia nervosa. Br Med J 2:477–478, 1974

5. Mitchell JE, Pyle RL, Miner RA: Gastric dilatation as a complication of bulimia. Psychosomatics 23:96–98, 1982

6. Mitikainen N: Spontaneous rupture of the stomach. Am J Surg 138:451–452, 1979

7. Friedman EJ: Death from ipecac intoxication in a patient with anorexia nervosa. Am J Psychiatry 141:702–703, 1984

8. Zucker S: Disturbances in cardiac rhythm in bulimia. Paper presented at the First International Conference on Eating Disorders. New York, April 1984

9. Mitchell JE, Pyle RL, Eckert ED, et al: Electrolyte and other physiological abnormalities in patients with bulimia. Psychol Med 13:273–278, 1983

10. Halmi KA, Falk JR: Common physiological changes in anorexia nervosa. International Journal of Eating Disorders 1:16–27, 1981

11. McArney ER: Rib fractures in anorexia nervosa. J Adolesc Health Care 4:40–43, 1983

12. Matthews BJ, Lacey JH: Skeletal maturation, growth hormone and nutritional status in anorexia nervosa. International Journal of Eating Disorders 2:145–150, 1983

13. Szmukler GI, Russell GFM: Diabetes mellitus, anorexia nervosa and bulimia. Am J Psychiatry 142:305–308, 1983

14. Hillard JR, Lobo MC, Keeling RP: Bulimia and diabetes: a potentially life-threatening combination. Psychosomatics 24:292–295, 1983

15. Mitchell JE, Bantle JP: Metabolic and endocrine investigations in women of normal weight with the bulimia syndrome. Biol Psychiatry 18:355–365, 1983

16. Gwirtsman HE, Roy-Byrne P, Yager J, et al: Neuroendocrine abnormalities in bulimia. Am J Psychiatry 140:559–563, 1983

17. Hudson JI, Pope HG, Jonas JM, et al: Hypothalamic-pituitary-adrenal-axis hyperactivity in bulimia. Psychiatry Res 8:111–117, 1983

4

The Outpatient Management of Bulimia

Joel Yager, M.D.
Carole K. Edelstein, M.D.

4

The Outpatient Management of Bulimia

The outpatient management of bulimia can involve a variety of psychological and medical strategies. The combination and sequence of interventions to be used with any given patient depends on factors related to the patient's clinical picture, the patient's ability and willingness to participate in a recommended treatment plan, and the availability of relevant resources such as qualified professionals and a way to pay for them. Comprehensive treatment planning starts with comprehensive assessment. This chapter will describe the necessary components of outpatient assessment for bulimia from which treatment decisions follow, and the various elements of outpatient intervention that may be integrated into any one patient's treatment plan.

Since other chapters in this volume cover group therapy, hospitalization, and medication treatment, we will comment only briefly on the details of those important aspects of comprehensive care and will focus primarily on psycho-educational and psychotherapeutic approaches. At the same time we will address the problem of integrating the different aspects of care.

ASSESSING THE PATIENT FOR TREATMENT

In formulating a treatment plan, the various intrapersonal and interpersonal settings in which bulimia is found must be taken into account. The bulimic behaviors themselves, which may be conceptualized as mechanisms for tension reduction, habits, or forms of self-destructive gratification, are found in a wide variety of people, who differ in their underlying biological and psychological makeups. A broad biopsychosocial concept of cause and treatment is necessary. In some patients, for example, the propensity for obesity is so great that the patient is likely to become obese unless an almost impossible degree of dietary restraint is constantly exerted. Some patients may develop bulimic behaviors only in certain bulimogenic social contexts, such as glamour-oriented sorority houses or weight-preoccupied athletic teams, and be able to give up these behaviors with reasonable ease when away from such environments. The recommendation of individual therapy, group therapy, medication, other interventions, or any combination of treatments has to be related to the clinical dimensions apparently relevant in any given patient's bulimia. Each dimension relates to specific therapeutic "receptor sites" and treatment strategies. The following major dimensions will influence individual treatment and must be assessed for any patient.

The Eating Symptoms Themselves

What are the bulimic symptoms, their frequency, intensity, and duration? Patients in our clinic have most frequently binged and purged at least daily, often several times each day, and rarely less than several times each week.

Is there any normal meal taking? Patients rarely eat normal meals when not binge-eating: they will eat very little or fast entirely, as if to compensate for the excessive eating during binges. Many patients eat little breakfast and minimal lunches, only to binge—averaging 2,000 to 5,000 calories or more per binge—starting in mid-afternoon or after dinner.

Has there been frank anorexia nervosa? What is the weight history, and what does the patient want to weigh? What eating rituals and irrational thoughts concerning eating and body image are present? The patient's desired weight and body image in relation to past weight history are critical. How realistic (and healthy) is the weight she desires, especially in relation to her own previous weight and her family's weight history?

To what extent does the patient use fasting, excessive exercise, laxatives, diet pills (what type), diuretics, or purgatives to assist in weight loss?

Psychological and Behavioral Dimensions

What are the intrapsychic, interpersonal, and situational prompters and inhibitors of these behaviors? What are the patient's understandings, beliefs, and insights into the reasons for and significance of the symptoms? To what extent are the eating binges and purging episodes acceptable and welcome pastimes, and to what extent are they seriously ego-alien? What are the associated irrational thoughts concerning eating, foods, body shape, and self-worth in relation to self-control and physical appearance? What is the patient's cognitive style, and to what extent are the thoughts about eating woven into tightly obsessional systems, or totally unavailable to the patient's conscious thoughts as in dissociated or split-off thinking?

At what level is the patient's psychosexual development? At what point, and in relation to what life events and developmental issues, did the bulimic symptoms appear? What kind of relationships does the patient have with family and other significant persons?

What are the behavioral and environmental aspects—that is, what is revealed by examination of the *antecedents, behaviors,* and *consequences* (the classic "ABCs") of the bulimic symptoms? What thoughts, feelings, images, and sensations are present before a binge is initiated? In what setting is binge-eating likely to be elicited? Some patients will relate eating binges to pre-existing feelings of tension-frustration, or boredom, or loneliness, or deprivation, or all of the above. Some patients eat continuously whenever they are at home near the refrigerator or pantry. Others will binge-eat just on weekends.

Similarly, the behaviors and rituals themselves are of concern. How much planning goes into the binges? When and where is the food obtained, and how is it paid for? Each of these elements carries an entry point for change. Where does the binge-eating take place? With whom? Many patients will binge-eat standing in front of their refrigerators. Others will, like some alcoholics, binge-eat in their cars to avoid being observed or found out.

What foods are preferred?

Following the binge, and also following the purge, what are the usual behaviors, feelings, and images: disgust? relief? remorse? relaxation?

Affective Dimensions

The majority of patients with bulimia are demoralized and despondent, have very low self-esteem, and feel very unsure of themselves. Some report symptoms usually associated with more severe depressions—hypersomnia or insomnia, suicidal thoughts, inability to concentrate or to function at work or school. But in any given person the extent to which these are symptoms of a secondary rather than a primary depression must be evaluated. Does the depression result from the patient's life being out of control with regard to eating? Or is the depression primarily related to biological vulnerabilities, unfortunate life events, inadequate coping with the issues of adolescence and young adulthood, and so forth? In the latter case, the bulimia might be viewed as symptoms elaborated in the wake of a primary depression.

Such linear causal formulations, however, are probably too simple, in light of the complex interweaving of the strands of affective and eating disorders in various family histories and in the individual's development. The debate as to whether bulimia is a "variant of affective disorder" is not just academic, since this formulation has been used as a basis for prescribing antidepressant medications to bulimic patients. The use of antidepressant medications as part of the overall treatment strategy has garnered advocates, but an understanding of the exact mechanisms of action of these drugs in bulimic patients, and of what such effects imply about the pathogenesis of these disorders, awaits further research.

Characterological Dimensions

Many patients with bulimia have serious character problems. Detailed histories and psychological test profiles often reveal severe trait as well as state personality problems. At least one-third of the patients seen in our clinic have very troubling and pervasive character problems. These include a shaky sense of self along with a constant search for others to provide direction and validation; an inability to know or to read one's own feeling states; great self-absorption and selfishness; impulsivity in decisions and actions concerning relationships, sexuality, work, and other key areas of living; and emotional lability, with extremes of idealization and vilification (1). Patients may have utterly unrealistic and magical fantasies about cures, and they find themselves devastated and angry when their expectations are not rapidly met.

Some character-related problems—for example, shoplifting—may be consequences of the bulimia, just as many "character problems" displayed by narcotics abusers and alcoholics appear to be consequences of the addictions, fading away when the addictive behaviors stop. Some of the problems may reflect arrested adolescent development, development that may proceed more normally once the bulimic syndrome abates.

Substance Abuse Dimensions

A small but important group of bulimic patients, less than 20 percent of those entering our clinic, have significant coexistent substance abuse problems, usually alcohol and/or cocaine abuse. These problems require urgent attention, usually taking priority over the bulimic symptoms.

Social and Family Dimensions

The social and interpersonal aspects of the symptoms are of importance. Where and with whom are bulimic episodes most, and least, likely to occur? Who knows about the behavior, what do they know, and how do they respond to the patient? How concerned are significant others with the patient's physical appearance, physical health, emotional well being, and individualization? Are significant figures supportive? Over-involved and unable to separate? Excessively and unremittingly harsh and critical?

Physical Health Dimensions

Medical problems associated with bulimia are described in detail in Chapter Three of this monograph. While these problems are ordinarily not of major consequence in the normal weight patient, they may be life threatening in the low weight bulimic—the patient who has had anorexia nervosa—primarily because of potential impairment of cardiac strength and conduction. Are other symptoms suggestive of weight loss or hyperactivity present, such as amenorrhea or oligomenorrhea? Does the patient have bowel complaints which may be related to laxative abuse? Fatigue and lassitude, which may be perceived as mental depression, may be due to hypokalemia or other physical conditions. What is the patient's thyroid status? The highly symptomatic vomiter and/or laxative abuser deserves a medical workup, as Halmi recommends.

Other Dimensions

Other dimensions requiring assessment are those personal and interpersonal factors most likely to affect participation in treatment: the patient's own belief systems about bulimia and what will make her better; the patient's past treatment history—what hasn't worked, and why; family and significant-other influences that prompt or may hamper treatment; the extent to which the patient can access care, including financial means, time available, proximity to care givers, and so forth; the reasons why the patient is presenting for treatment now; and the strength of current motivations for change.

Chapter 4

GENERAL ASPECTS OF TREATMENT
PLANNING FOR BULIMIA

The literature on treatment for bulimia contains many contradictions, and important questions have not yet been resolved. No one method has yet proven more effective than all the others in the treatment of all bulimic patients. Some literature is available in support of each of the following modalities: cognitive-behavioral-feminist group therapy alone; individual cognitive-behavioral therapy; combined individual and group cognitive-behavioral therapy; group therapy in conjunction with individual therapy and various medications; medication more or less alone (that is, with little additional *formal* support). Successful one-to-one psychodynamic therapy has been described in small series. Family therapy and self-help groups have been proposed as the sole therapeutic modalities or as useful adjuncts. And we can be sure that other types of therapies will be touted in the future. Furthermore, studies often report patients successfully entered into their brand of treatment who previously failed others; patients successfully treated with behavioral or medication therapy who were previously unsuccessfully treated with psychodynamically oriented therapies; patients who failed on medication A who responded to medication B, and vice versa.

Recall also that only those patients who fail one treatment apply for a second modality, and that many patients successfully or unsuccessfully treated with all types of treatments are not written up. A preliminary analysis of data we have collected on satisfaction with various treatments bears mention. Among 246 women (drawn from a national survey) who met *DSM-III* criteria for bulimia, various treatments—including psychodynamic individual, group behavioral, and so forth—yielded comparable degrees of satisfaction, with relatively minor variation. Only about one-sixth of the respondents were "very satisfied" with any modality, and about two-fifths were "somewhat satisfied" (2). To add additional perspective, we have seen more than a few patients who at the right moment in their lives stopped chronic, severe bulimic behaviors on their own, by sheer will power *without* professional treatment specifically aimed at this disorder. As with smoking, drinking, and obesity, with proper motivation and resolve, substantial numbers of people may be able by themselves to put an end to their symptomatic behaviors and experience attendant psychological benefits. We do not know the percentages or characteristics of bulimic persons capable of such "spontaneous" cures. But if a treatment study includes many such highly motivated patients who are on the verge of spontaneous remission, the treatment is likely to produce good results. On the other hand, if a study starts with an unselected group of patients who have failed with other modalities, results are less likely to be good unless the treatment offered is genuinely effective.

Does surrendering bulimic behavior simply constitute a superficial "flight into health"? Few patients harbor the illusion that all their problems are resolved with the disappearance of bulimic symptoms. Yet, virtually all would agree that associated problems of affect, self-esteem, and social relationships not only improve but are more profitably examined and dealt with once the bulimic behaviors per se have abated.

TREATMENT DECISIONS

Given the current state of the art, what combinations of strategies are most sensible for which patients? For each patient a series of decisions must be made, of which a major one is whether the patient should be hospitalized. In our experience, and in Fairburn's (3), hospitalization for bulimia is indicated in the following situations:

1. The patient has failed ordinarily effective outpatient treatment and continues to experience health-damaging symptoms with severe electrolyte or cardiac problems.
2. A medication trial is indicated, but adequate monitoring or compliance is unlikely as an outpatient.
3. The patient is suicidal.

Specifics of hospital management are considered in detail in

Chapter Six, by Gwirtsman and colleagues. What remains un-known is the impact of hospitalization. We have seen some pa-tients consolidate and retain the symptomatic gains made during hospitalization if they continue in outpatient treatment, but in others we have also seen symptoms return rapidly following dis-charge. At the time of this writing no systematic follow-up studies have been reported concerning either the short-term or long-term efficacy of hospital treatment for bulimia.

If a decision against hospitalization has been made, then the next question is, what outpatient therapies should be used? The types of therapies offered are inevitably determined by 1) the caregiver's views of what the symptoms represent (for example, defenses, breakthroughs of impulses, habits) and of how therapeu-tic change occurs; and 2) the types of therapy with which the patient will cooperate and in which the patient has the capacity to profitably engage. Current information suggests that psychody-namic, behavioral, group, and family therapies, as well as medica-tion, can all contribute to successful treatment.

Psychodynamic Psychotherapy

The literature on the purely psychodynamic psychotherapy of bulimia is heavily anecdotal (4,5). It is fair to say that psychody-namically oriented psychotherapy, which usually includes many subtle behavioral components, has not yet been systematically studied for the treatment of bulimia. Nevertheless, many authori-ties believe that comprehensive treatment programs for bulimia should include aspects of insight-oriented psychotherapy. In our experience at UCLA, patients often preferentially request individ-ual therapy with a strong psychodynamic component, regardless of the other aspects of treatment.

The issues to be considered in psychodynamic therapy include those commonly seen with late adolescent and young adult women: relations with and emancipation from family, friendships and intimacies, loneliness, femininity, physical appearance and its importance, personal goals and values, role confusion, frustrating tensions and releases, trust in one's own judgment, need for control, feelings of impotence, and the like.

Indications for a psychodynamic approach include assessments that the issues described above are of significance and linked to the initiation *and* maintenance of the bulimic symptoms, and that the patient has some capacity to introspect. The patient's personality, cognitive style, motivation, curiosity, flexibility, and perspective on the nature of the mind and the therapeutic relationship will determine where the therapy will lie along the supportive-exploratory continuum, and how active and confrontative or gently passive the therapist will be in various phases of treatment. For example, the shy, withdrawn, avoidant patient may not only need a longer time than others to develop trust but may have to be virtually led by the hand to face the issues. The impulsive, acting-out patient may require confrontation and a firm setting of limits. The highly motivated, psychologically minded patient may need a therapist who knows when to be quiet and let her do her own psychological work, without interfering or sidetracking her. The patient who, in a conflictual interpersonal situation, is unable to recognize what she feels, or denies having feelings she can grasp, or too readily accepts another person's description of what she is feeling while disowning her own appraisal, should not be told how she "must be feeling" by the therapist; such a patient needs to gain some perspective on what problems prevent her from knowing, or sensing, or accepting her own feelings in the first place.

Common transference themes include those related to the therapist as various parental figures who are harsh and stern, or gullible and manipulable, or overly demanding; as idealized successful woman figures (who may simultaneously evoke feelings in the patient that she will never be nearly as good or amount to anything); as men who are objects for infatuation or seduction, or who are sources of frightening intimacy and rejection, or who are selfish and insensitive.

Countertransference issues include those commonly evoked by adolescent and early adult women, who may be chronically demoralized, or impulsive and acting out, or attractive and sexual, and who may not respond symptomatically in as rapid a fashion as the therapist would like.

In our view, it is necessary for the psychodynamically oriented therapist to *attend* to the eating disorder symptoms per se and to hold out clear expectations for change. For several reasons, we do *not* believe that the therapist should assume that the symptoms will fade away by themselves after the underlying conflicts are all cleared up. First, the underlying conflicts and issues may not be satisfactorily resolved within a reasonable period of time in spite of the best efforts of the therapist and patient. Second, the symptoms themselves, no doubt, generate many problems in their wake, such as low self-esteem and feelings of being out of control, problems that may be alleviated once the symptoms are interrupted. Third, the goal of symptom change per se is usually of great importance to the patient—and to the therapist as well—and is not to be minimized.

Most important, every psychodynamic psychotherapy contains cognitive and behavioral elements—the altered perspectives and insights imparted by the therapists, sometimes forcefully, designed as cognitive alternatives, and the therapists' prompts and approvals constituting behavioral contingencies. Therefore, the question is not *whether* to use psychodynamic or cognitive-behavioral therapy but *how* to design a therapy containing the aspects of all these approaches that will be most useful therapeutically. There is certainly no current evidence to suggest that combined approaches are less effective than those that are of theoretically "purer" culture. With this in mind we can turn to an examination of cognitive and behavioral elements in psychotherapy.

Cognitive and Behavioral Psychotherapies

Cognitive-behavior modification in combination with insight-oriented discussions may be more useful than psychodynamic therapies alone for bulimic disorders. Such therapies have previously been described for obese patients (6–8), for patients with anorexia nervosa (9), and more recently for patients with bulimia (10–13).

In one of the first published papers in this area Fairburn described the treatment of 11 patients who had been bulimic for an average of four years. Five of them previously had anorexia nervosa (10). The patients were treated individually for an average of seven months. At the start of treatment, Fairburn focused on helping the patients to control food and eating; later he examined their broader coping strategies, using cognitive therapy techniques for a wide range of problems. Treatment consisted of two phases. Phase one lasted about eight weeks, during which patients were seen two to three times a week, kept a detailed behavioral diary that included all their eating behaviors, were educated about bulimia, and were put on a rigid eating schedule. The family was often seen as well. In Fairburn's view, once eating was regulated, vomiting often disappeared by itself. In phase two, patients were taught new ways to cope. Throughout treatment, patients regulated their own food intake and neither outside controls nor medications were used. By the end of treatment nine of the 11 patients stopped bingeing and vomiting entirely, and they maintained this improvement at follow-up, conducted on the average almost a year later. At that time, most of the patients had gained a few pounds but were handling this well.

More classical behavior therapies for bulimia employ techniques such as self-monitoring, targeting, graphing, stimulus control, and both positive and negative reinforcements (14–17). These therapies usually entail 12 to 40 sessions over three to 10 months. Typically, improvement was reported as maintained in follow-ups of nine to 12 months.

But, what are the specific therapeutic factors in these treatments? How ready were these patients to change at the start? What credit should go to the excellent relationships they developed with highly involved, well-informed, active therapists? As with psychodynamically oriented psychotherapies, there is much variation in how cognitive-behavior therapy is conducted: in the therapist's skills in selecting and applying the right cognitive and behavioral elements with a given patient, the patient's willingness to cooperate with the procedures, and other clinical and motivational factors.

To summarize, several uncontrolled series have demonstrated that many patients treated individually with cognitive and behavioral therapies have reduced or eliminated eating binges and vomiting. Based on current practices of clinicians at major treatment centers, the following components of therapy should be strongly considered for any patient's treatment:

1. *Diary and journal keeping.* These activities may help the patient to develop increased awareness—an observing ego, if you will—regarding the details of binges and purges, together with their antecedents and consequences. Some patients are reassured by the structure and are enthusiastic about keeping diaries. However, others experience diary-keeping as childish and demanding. As with other symptomatic behaviors, such as enuresis, the very attention and discipline required to keep a diary may be therapeutic and may help to bring about a reduction in symptom frequency. In one medication study the requirement of keeping a daily diary (used in both control and active groups) did not result in an increase in symptom-free days (18), but a combination of encouragement and diary-keeping often appears to be useful. Patients frequently find satisfaction in precisely recording increasing numbers of binge-free and purge-free days, in graphing a concrete visual record of their improvement.

   In our experience and that of others, diaries are most likely to be taken seriously if they are provided to the patients as preprinted booklets; patients asked to create their own are more inclined to cut corners in compliance. Elements to be recorded in printed diaries usually include day/date, and for each episode of eating (normal meals, snacks, binges) the quantities, types of food, and physical and social setting, whether alone or with others (and with whom), and antecedent, concurrent, and consequent emotions, thoughts and behaviors (13). Also recorded are associated pertinent behaviors such as exercise and the use of medications, drugs, or alcohol. The sessions with the therapist should devote some time to a review and discussion of such diaries so that keeping them up remains a rewarding experience rather than a sterile exercise for the patient.

2. *Normal, planned eating.* Many bulimic patients suffer from "dietary chaos" and rarely eat normal meals, essentially starving themselves when they aren't binge-eating. As patients start to add normal, higher calorie breakfasts and lunches to their diets, a practice we strongly insist upon from the start, many find it easier to resist binge-eating later in the day. Some patients require relatively rigid meal programs at the start, to minimize the threat they experience when confronted with dietary overchoice. Consultations and educational readings are necessary. Some patients are quite ignorant about basic nutritional requirements. Providing them with sound information such as that contained in *Jane Brody's Nutrition Book* (19) and in some readily available calorie counters—for example, Kraus's (20)—can be useful.

3. *Education about bulimia.* Patients should learn what is currently known about the nature and treatment of bulimia. To be encouraging, we provide new patients with many accounts of others who have done well, discussing how and why they improved. We recommend several popular books about bulimia such as those by Cauwels (21) and by Squire (22), and we also suggest that patients join some of the national eating disorders self-help organizations and read their regularly published newsletters (See Appendix of this chapter).

4. *Analysis of patient's beliefs and attitudes.* The therapist assists the patient in identifying distorted cognitions, self-defeating states of mind, and faulty assumptions. In addition to specific issues around bulimic behaviors, body images, and weight preoccupation, important other areas for review are those previously mentioned in the section on psychodynamic therapy. Many of the faulty assumptions are similar to those described for patients with anorexia nervosa (9) and depression (23).

Magical thinking, superstitious thinking, "all or none" thinking, and magnification and minimization of certain ideas and beliefs are seen frequently. Common distortions are

related to the following areas: 1) Belief that a calorie of carbohydrate differs a great deal from a calorie of fat; that a calorie
of sugar differs from a calorie of starch; that it is healthier to
eat far more protein than carbohydrate; that restrictive elimination of certain foods is virtuous; that "full" means "fatter."
2) Self-control: Belief that giving in to any restricted food *has*
to precipitate a binge; that self-control in eating is necessarily
related to self-control in other areas of life, such as work,
school, and sex; that self-control in eating throughout life can
be obtained only through an ultra-rigid diet plan. 3) Self-
image: Many dislike all or parts of their bodies (general or
specific dysmorphophobias); equate self-worth with physical
appearance; are certain that minimal weight shifts are obvious
to everybody; believe that their bulimia is proof of all-perva-
sive moral and character defects; and feel that they deserve to
be belittled and debased.

5. *Cognitive and insight-based corrections of distorted beliefs.*
   Techniques include interpretation, confrontation, distancing,
   externalization, thought stopping, substitution, and related
   strategies. Realistic weight and body-image goals should be
   developed.

   Unrealistic beliefs are challenged; their origins are uncovered and put into perspective as having human (and therefore
   challengeable) sources; alternative self-statements are developed and rehearsed. Humor can be used to provide philosophi-
   cal points of view that counter unrealistic needs for perfection,
   ascetic restriction, and rigidity. The punch lines of jokes often
   provide cognitive self-statements that can counteract over-
   serious, self-punitive, restrictive beliefs.

6. *Substitution of alternative gratifications and coping mechanisms for tension reduction.* The therapist can introduce more
   adaptive direct methods of conflict resolution and problem
   solving than the patient has previously used. The aim is to
   enable patients to cope more directly with their problems so
   that tensions previously discharged through binge-eating may
   be averted. A large number of substitute activities, such as
   exercise or scheduled social events, may be helpful (24).

Coping skills are strengthened: Some patients require training in being able to sense their inner feelings, needs, values, and priorities before they can act adaptively upon them. For example, one patient only slowly and reluctantly permitted herself to recognize how lonely she felt; in response she first bought a dog as a companion while at the same time she set about developing better human relationships. Other patients require training in how to communicate more effectively, or to be constructively assertive, or to be less ineffective and destructive with their anger. Role plays and rehearsals in therapy sessions are useful; sometimes elaborate word-for-word scripts need to be developed for the patient to carry out to real-life situations.

7. *Analysis and alteration or control of symptom-promoting environmental contingencies (space, time, and people).* This approach has been effective in behaviorally oriented weight-reduction programs. Time of day, the presence of certain others, and other specific elements may constitute binge-evoking or binge-inhibiting stimuli (12, 13).

For example, if binges are most likely to occur following time spent with a certain person, the precise associated stimuli are uncovered and changed, or the person is avoided. If being at home alone on weekends elicits the symptoms, additional efforts are made to get out with others. If inadequate sleep and fatigue are often a prelude to binge-eating, care is taken to obtain adequate rest. Some therapists ask their patients to schedule programmed eating binges during unusual times or in unusual places, as a means of co-opting resistances and of breaking up some of the habitual behavior sequences associated with the binge episodes.

8. *Contracts.* Both positive and negative rewards have been useful. *Positive rewards,* over and above those of simply getting better, may help if the initial incentive to improve is high and the rewards are meaningful. To illustrate, one patient found buying a new blouse after each week that she met her goals to be a successful reward; another patient, a woman who binged and purged multiple times each day, benefited from a program

in which she made a long-distance phone call to a special friend following each binge-free day.

A negative contingency program may be considered for the recalcitrant patient, as it is with alcohol and drug abusers, but only if the therapist has an excellent relationship with the patient and genuinely believes that the patient is fully capable of making the planned degree of change. Proposed negative contingencies should never put the patient in the position of having to perform self-destructive or immoral acts, but they should be sufficiently powerful to assure success. The patient's self-esteem must be carefully supported throughout.

For one patient, who in our view had the capacity to change but failed to improve with conventional psychodynamic and behavioral therapies, and who refused medication, sufficient incentive was provided in the following manner. She agreed to compose a letter informing a friend about her bulimia. The patient wrote the letter and handed it to the therapist with the understanding that the therapist would mail it if the patient failed to meet weekly goals for improvement. The patient would have been greatly embarrassed if the letter had been sent, and she did not doubt the therapist's resolve. With this program her daily binge and purge rituals stopped entirely within two weeks, and she remained free of symptoms (although she gained about 10 pounds) in follow-up of a year and half, confirmed by her family.

With another patient the negative contingency plan required the patient to send a campaign donation to one of her least favorite political candidates each time she failed to meet her goals. That plan was also successful. But great care must be taken to assure that such plans are initiated at the right time, and that they have the patient's full cooperation.

9. *Psychological immunization about persistent food preoccupation and periodic backsliding.* Patients should be informed that food preoccupation often persists even after binge-eating and purging behaviors stop, so that they don't interpret such thoughts as failures or use them to justify giving in to cravings. Similarly, patients should be informed that small

episodes of backsliding, which are not uncommon, need not herald an avalanche. Relapse-prevention training has been effective for similar addictive problems (25, 26) and ordinarily involves anticipatory cognitive restructuring.

10. *Mental imagery techniques.* Such techniques often help patients to bypass obsessional, intellectualized defenses and frequently generate unexpected new perspectives about the meanings and significance of their symptoms in relation to ongoing life situations (27). Imagery has been particularly beneficial for some adolescents and young adult patients who are still forming their identities. In the course of imagery work some patients have become better able to surrender their symptoms, after more strongly experiencing them as ego-alien developmental immaturities.

Should Group Therapy Be Used?

Group psychotherapies that combine psychodynamic and behavior techniques have been widely used in the treatment of bulimia, at least adjunctively, and in some instances successfully as the sole treatment modality. The empirical data base upon which this popularity rests is small but growing, and is discussed in detail in Chapter Five of this monograph.

Several programs, such as those described by Dixon and Kiecolt-Glaser (28), Lacey (29), and our group at UCLA (30), have combined individual and group therapy. Recognizing that what we recommend is based on clinical impressions that will have to be validated or modified by systematic research, our remarks about group therapy will be limited to indications for its use and its combination with individual therapy.

To start, in an analysis of follow-up data from about 200 women who are part of a national sample with self-reported eating disorders, we found that their satisfaction with the psychotherapies in general could best be described as moderate or modest. Satisfaction with all therapies was generally greater among those whose symptoms were less severe, and patients with less severe symptoms tended to rate group therapy as slightly more beneficial than individual therapy. In contrast, patients with more severe symptoms viewed individual therapy as relatively more valuable than group therapy (31). These preliminary findings should not be interpreted as supporting an "either-or" recommendation for treatment. In almost all cases, we have found that if practical considerations permit the patient to undertake *both* individual and group therapy, she will gain from both. The group support and interaction with other recovering bulimics appear to be beneficial regardless of the theoretical orientation of the leader.

If only *one* therapy is possible, "healthier" patients may benefit from group alone to a greater extent than will those with a greater burden of pathology. For the sicker patients, individual therapy should be offered, to be supplemented when appropriate by group therapy. Further, in our view, when a patient in group therapy alone is not doing well, a fresh rethinking of the case is indicated, often with the addition of individual therapy. And the addition of group therapy should be among the considerations for the patient who is not progressing in individual treatment.

Frequent communication is necessary between group therapists and individual therapists. Some patients have a tendency to reveal essential aspects of themselves only in one treatment setting and not in the other. Although some patients may want to keep the two treatment situations totally separate from each other, we believe that the patient should be informed at the outset that the therapists will communicate with each other to share information and to develop an integrated approach to care of the patient. Ordinarily, patients greatly appreciate this evidence of extra concern and effort on the part of the therapists.

In our experience, patients with major problems of impulsivity and other borderline character features should not be started in a group immediately, and never without concurrent individual therapy. Without adequate preparation, such patients often have difficulty in sustaining constructive group participation, and after a few meetings they may leave disruptively. We therefore insist that such patients start with a "trial" of individual therapy alone before being referred into a group, even in cases where the patient has come to our clinic specifically seeking group treatment. After one to two months, the individual therapist is better able to gauge the patient's staying power and suitability for group.

What Is the Role of Family Therapy?

Indications for family therapy with bulimic patients include the following: 1) The patient is living or highly entangled with her over-involved family of origin, a family in which everyone means well but in which chronic unresolved conflicts appear to fuel and sustain the bulimia and related symptoms. 2) A parent or spouse constantly belittles and undermines the patient and her attempts to improve. 3) Family members actively seek information and guidance as to how they can best support and help the patient.

Issues that require attention in family therapy often include distorted and misdirected concerns; ineffective communications; covert and overt conflicts about roles, values, needs, and expectations among family members (especially those related to separation-individuation and mutual dependency needs); and other issues related to the specific developmental tasks of each family member and of the family as a whole.

With younger patients, such as adolescents living at home with the family of origin, a family assessment is indicated in every case. With the young adult who lives away from home, the need to see the whole family may be less pressing but is still often self-evident early in treatment. In our clinic, for a sizable number of patients sustained improvement would be virtually impossible without concurrent involvement of the family.

A full discussion of the tactics of family therapy for bulimia is beyond the scope of this chapter but is available elsewhere (32). Briefly, we often find concurrent individual and family (or couple) therapy to be more valuable than individual therapy alone. Depending on the skills of the therapist and beliefs of the patient, therapy can be successfully conducted with either the same therapist seeing both the patient individually and the family (or couple), or by having different therapists for the individual and family work. Our own preference, in the service of reducing confusion, is to have the same therapist work with both individual and family whenever possible. In our experience, we have *not* found family therapy alone, in the absence of individual therapy, to be of any particular advantage in the treatment of bulimia.

In our clinic several short-term multiple family groups have been conducted, usually scheduled for six weekly sessions; each session involves from three to six families or part-families, including the patients. The groups are quasi-didactic but inevitably include consciousness-raising, comparisons, confrontations, sharing of dilemmas and strategies, and a sense of mutual purpose. Virtually all participants have praised them as extremely worthwhile, and monthly follow-up groups have been arranged at the requests of group members. However, no study has yet been conducted to assess systematically the relative contributions that family therapy or family group therapy can make toward an overall treatment plan.

What Is the Role of Medication?

Since the final chapter, by Pope and colleagues, discusses in detail the use of medication for bulimia, our comments will be limited to observations on selecting patients for medication, interpreting the effects sometimes attributed to medication, and integrating medication treatment with other aspects of care. The literature in this area has been growing rapidly, and the safest statement that can be made at present is that *some* medications offer *some* promise for *some* patients (33–40). Each medication has its own advocates and theoretical rationale for why it may work in bulimia, but proper selection criteria have not been established. Nor is it clear how much placebo, antitension, antidepressant, anticonvulsant, and other properties of the medications each play a role in producing therapeutic effects.

What is clear are the following:

1. Many patients are unwilling to take any medication at all. Although the recent upsurge in magazine articles and popular books describing the potential benefits of medication in the

treatment of bulimia has led to increasing numbers of patients coming to our clinic *seeking* medication treatment, a large number remain who are skittish about medication use. They may believe that their problems are exclusively psychogenic and that it is morally superior to engage in "talking therapy" that might enable them to conquer the problem through their "own efforts," rather than to take medication; they may fear that a reliance on medication implies that they are biologically defective; they may fear becoming dependent on a medication; they may fear acute or potential side effects of medication on alertness, coordination, or pregnancy.

In our opinion such patients should always start out with a trial of intensive psychological therapies; a reasonable number are likely to get better without drugs in a reasonable period of time (39). However, if the patient presents strong concurrent indications for medication such as a major depressive disorder and positive family history, or severe cyclothymia, or epileptoid symptoms, the physician should energetically educate the patient about medication (which may include providing appropriate articles or books).

2. Even for the patient who is *not* obviously depressed, a recent double-blind study suggests that desipramine may be more helpful than placebo (38). Therefore, in our view *any* patient who after several months fails to show improvement with psychological therapies alone should be considered for a medication trial.

3. Some patients appear to respond positively to medications almost as soon as they take the first tablet, certainly before any significant blood levels have been achieved. Such patients may be placebo responders. For them, we suggest supportively withdrawing medication after a relatively brief trial, with the expectation that the therapeutic improvements will be sustained.

4. Some patients respond positively to medications such as tricyclic antidepressants or monoamine oxidase inhibitors after just a few days, before the usual antidepressant effect would ordinarily be expected. Placebo effects may be at work here, too. But in such cases the medications may also be exerting their

effects as antitension/anti-anxiety agents rather than as classic antidepressants or placebos.

5. In our experience, bulimic patients who require medication do best when they are also in psychotherapy. This is in accord with the observations of Weissman et al. regarding the treatment of depressed outpatients who also did best with combined treatment (41). While medication may give the patient some symptom and mood relief, persistent cognitive distortions, developmental arrests, and family conflicts are less likely simply to disappear without psychotherapy. For such cases we usually recommend some sort of combined treatment—for example, medication plus individual psychotherapy, or medication plus group, or medication plus both (most commonly).

6. However, some patients are *not* very psychologically minded, *do* want and need medication, and cannot afford multiple modalities. For such patients a medication trial at the outset with careful medical follow-up (visits each week or two), without separate "psychotherapy," may be tried *if* in the physician's judgment the patient will be responsible about taking medications and will not act out around them. But if after several weeks the patient's progress is unsatisfactory, a reconsideration of the case is required, just as for the patient who fails to respond to psychotherapy alone. In these instances, other combinations of different medications, individual therapy, and group therapy may need to be added.

CONCLUSION

Studies and clinical experiences discussed in this chapter and elsewhere in this monograph suggest that patients may be helped substantially by different combinations of cognitive-behavioral-psychodynamic treatment individually, in groups, with medication, and with the adjunctive use of family therapy. Perhaps virtually *any* treatment modality will work for less disturbed patients who are ready to change. But many of the research studies excluded difficult patients with severe character problems or concurrent anorexia nervosa—patients whose bulimia often resists successful treatment with *any* of the current approaches. Further research is necessary to better determine which patients are best treated by which treatments, and to develop effective treatments for those patients for whom available treatments are ineffective.

Until such research is completed, treatment plans, to some extent, must be "educated trial-and-error," as described above. There is no evidence that combinations of therapeutic approaches are harmful to one another, and there is some suggestion that various therapies may have additive or synergistic benefits. The belief systems and prejudices of the patient and therapist will largely determine the initial treatment strategies to be used. However, as with all clinical problems, if a patient does not show improvement within a reasonable period of time—usually two months for bulimics—the treatment plan should be rethought. At that time additional therapeutic elements may be added and some of the initial ones modified or deleted, to maximize the likelihood of improvement. Problems arise when physicians are more strongly wedded to their loyalties to a particular treatment modality than they are to the goal of getting the patient better.

References

1. Mitchell JE, Pyle RL: The bulimic syndrome in normal weight individuals: a review. International Journal of Eating Disorders 1:61–73, 1982

2. Yager J, Landsverk J, Lee-Benner K, et al: Bulimia spectrum disorder: the Glamour survey. Paper presented at the 136th Annual Meeting of the American Psychiatric Association, New York, May 1983

3. Fairburn C: Binge eating and its management. Br J Psychiatry 141:631–633, 1982

4. Bruch H: Eating Disorders: Obesity, Anorexia Nervosa and the Person Within. New York, Basic Books, 1973

5. Wilson CP: Fear of Being Fat: The Treatment of Anorexia Nervosa and Bulimia. New York, Jason Aronson, 1983

6. Stuart RB, Davis B: Slim Chance in a Fat World. Champaign, Ill, Research Press, 1972

7. Mahoney M, Mahoney K: Permanent Weight Control. New York, WW Norton, 1976

8. Meichenbaum D: Cognitive-Behavior Modification. New York, Plenum Press, 1977

9. Garner D, Garfinkel P, Bemis KM: A multidimensional psychotherapy for anorexia nervosa. International Journal of Eating Disorders 1:3–46, 1982

10. Fairburn C: A cognitive behavioral approach to the treatment of bulimia. Psychol Med 11:707–711, 1981

11. Fairburn, CG: Bulimia: its epidemiology and management. Psychiatric Annals 13:953–961, 1983

12. Orleans CT: Bulimarexia: guidelines for behavioral assessment and treatment, in The Binge-Purge Syndrome. Edited by Hawkins RC. New York, Springer, 1984

13. Loro AD Jr: Binge eating: a cognitive-behavioral treatment approach, in The Binge-Purge Syndrome. Edited by Hawkins RC. New York, Springer, 1984

14. Long CG, Cordle CJ: Psychological treatment of binge eating and self-induced vomiting. Br J Med Psychol 55:139–145, 1982

15. Rosen JC, Leitenberg H: Bulimia nervosa: treatment with exposure and response prevention. Behav Ther 13:117–124, 1982

16. Kenny FT, Solyom L: The treatment of compulsive vomiting through faradic disruption of mental images. Can Med Assoc J 105:1071–1073, 1971

17. Greenberg D, Marks I: Behavioral psychotherapy of uncommon referrals. Br J Psychiatry 141:148–153, 1982

18. Sabine EJ, Yonace A, Farrington AJ, et al: Bulimia nervosa: a placebo controlled, double-blind therapeutic trial of mianserin. Br J Clin Pharmacol 15:1955–2025, 1983

19. Brody JE: Jane Brody's Nutrition Book. New York, WW Norton, 1981

20. Kraus B: Calories and Carbohydrates. New York, New American Library, 1981

21. Cauwels JM: Bulimia: The Binge-Purge Compulsion. New York, Doubleday, 1983

22. Squire S: The Slender Balance: Causes and Cures for Bulimia, Anorexia and the Weight Loss/Weight Gain Seesaw. New York, GP Putnam, 1983

23. Beck AT: Cognitive Therapy and the Emotional Disorders. New York, International Universities Press, 1976

24. Merzer M: Winning the Diet Wars: A Rescue Plan for Those Who Love to Eat. New York, Harcourt, Brace, Jovanovich, 1980

25. Cummings C, Gordon JR, Marlatt GA: Relapse: prevention and prediction, in The Addictive Behaviors. Edited by Miller WR. New York, Pergamon Press, 1980

26. Marlatt GA, Gordon JR: Relapse Prevention. New York, Guilford Press, 1984

27. Kosbab PF: Imagery techniques in psychiatry. Arch Gen Psychiatry 31:283–290, 1974

28. Dixon KN, Kiecolt-Glaser J: An integrated group therapy approach to bulimia. Paper presented at the 134th Annual Meeting of the American Psychiatric Association, New Orleans, May 1981

29. Lacey JH: Bulimia nervosa, binge-eating, and psychogenic vomiting: a controlled treatment study and long-term outcome. Br Med J 286:1609–1613, 1983

30. Roy-Byrne P, Lee-Benner K, Yager J: Group therapy for bulimia: a year's experience. International Journal of Eating Disorders 3:97–116, 1984

31. Yager J, Landsverk J, Lee-Benner K, et al: Help seeking and satisfaction in bulimia. Paper presented at the 137th Annual Meeting of the American Psychiatric Association, Los Angeles, May 1984

32. Yager J, Strober M: Family aspects of eating disorders, in Psychiatry Update: The American Psychiatric Association Annual Review, Volume 4. Edited by Hales RE, Frances AJ. Washington, DC, American Psychiatric Press, 1985

33. Green RS, Rau JH: The use of diphenylhydantoin in compulsive eating disorders: further studies, in Anorexia Nervosa. Edited by Vigersky R. New York, Raven Press, 1977

34. Wermuth BM, Davis KL, Hollister LE, et al: Phenytoin treatment of the binge-eating syndrome. Am J Psychiatry 134:1249–1252, 1977

35. Kaplan AS, Garfinkel PA, Darby PL, et al: Carbamazepine in the treatment of bulimia. Am J Psychiatry 140:1225–1226, 1983

36. Walsh BT, Stewart JW, Wright L, et al: Treatment of bulimia with monoamine oxidase inhibitors. Am J Psychiatry 139:1629–1630, 1982

37. Pope HG Jr, Hudson JI, Jonas JM, et al: Bulimia treated with imipramine: a placebo-controlled, double-blind study. Am J Psychiatry 140:554–558, 1983

38. Hughes PL, Wells LA, Cunningham CJ, et al: Treating bulimia with desipramine: a double-blind placebo-controlled study. Paper presented at the 137th Annual Meeting of the American Psychiatric Association. Los Angeles, May 1984

39. Mitchell JE, Groat R: A placebo-controlled, double-blind trial of amitryptyline in bulimia. J Clin Psychopharmacol 4:186–193, 1984

40. Hsu LKG: Treatment of bulimia with lithium. Am J Psychiatry 141:1260–1262, 1984

41. Weissman MM, Klerman GL, Prusoff BA, et al: Depressed outpatients one year after treatment with drugs or interpersonal psychotherapy. Arch Gen Psychiatry 38:51–55, 1981

APPENDIX

Major national self-help organizations include:

1. Anorexia Nervosa and Related Eating Disorders (ANRED)
P.O. Box 5102
Eugene, Oregon 97405

2. Anorexia Nervosa and Associated Disorders (ANAD)
P.O. Box 271
Highland Park, Illinois 60035

3. National Anorexic Aid Society (NAAS)
P.O. Box 29651
Columbus, Ohio 43229

4. American Anorexia Nervosa Association (AANA)
133 Cedar Lane
Teaneck, New Jersey 07666

Others are developing, and small self-help groups are available in many communities. Several chapters of Overeaters Anonymous, a national weight reduction group modeled after Alcoholics Anonymous, have formed subgroups for bulimics called "Vomiters Anonymous."

5

Psychotherapy of Bulimia: The Role of Groups

Richard L. Pyle, M.D.
James E. Mitchell, M.D.

5

Psychotherapy of Bulimia: The Role of Groups

As previous chapters have reported, the eating disorder bulimia may have serious physical and social consequences (1-3). Although many individuals who have the bulimia syndrome may not seek treatment (4), reports on the high prevalence of bulimia in college mental health clinics (5), in student populations (6), and in nonstudent populations (7, 8) have identified a large pool of potential patients with this disorder. Group psychotherapy potentially offers a cost-effective approach for the large numbers of young women who are seeking treatment for bulimia. Initial pilot studies of the use of group psychotherapy in bulimia have been sufficiently favorable to warrant more rigorous research to investigate its efficacy.

The sudden increase in the number of patients seeking treatment for bulimia in the late 1970s, when there was little or no published data on bulimia treatment, led clinicians to examine treatment methods for related disorders to find effective techniques. Although the anorexia nervosa treatment literature supported the use of behavioral approaches (9), the surreptitious nature of bulimia and the absence of measurable responses such as weight gain made the use of specific operant reinforcement techniques problematic. However, reports of behavioral techniques for the treatment of obesity (10, 11) were more encouraging and suggested many ways to reduce the desire to binge-eat. Concurrently, examination of treatment models for disorders such as chemical dependency and overeating (Alcoholics Anonymous and Overeaters Anonymous) suggested that group approaches might be of value. Cognitive group therapy also received considerable attention because of its economy and effectiveness, particularly for patients with depression (12). The first published report on psychotherapy for "bulimarexia" noted that group treatment had the advantage of reducing feelings of isolation in bulimic patients (13). Subsequently, many group programs have incorporated techniques developed in the context of individual therapy, such as the intensive individual cognitive behavioral approach of Fairburn (14) and exposure and response prevention as described by Rosen and Leitenberg (15, 16).

Several attributes of group psychotherapy offer specific benefits for the treatment of bulimia. Group treatment may provide sufficient structure and support to: permit interruption of the chronic habitual nature of the behavior; promote reduction of the social isolation and loneliness which accompany the bulimia syndrome; greatly increase the number of people offering insight and support regarding the behavior; and permit group members to increase their own self-esteem by assisting other group members. Even though clinicians may not recommend outpatient group therapy for some patients (17, 18), there are few specific contraindications. Medical instability, current abuse of alcohol and drugs, or a weight 25 percent below the ideal weight for height and age are considered indications for inpatient care (19, 20). In addition, physicians who are evaluating bulimic patients should pay close attention to symptoms of other possible contraindications, such as an active psychosis, borderline personality disorder, major depression, the potential for suicide, major medical instability, severe laxative abuse, and the inability to maintain weight prior to or during the outpatient treatment program.

Since research on the effectiveness of group psychotherapy for bulimia is still in its infancy, issues relating to treatment definition, such as the general approach to be used, the treatment format, the optimal expectations for change, the type and number of therapists, and the criteria for selecting clients, have not been systematically investigated. Some group efforts reported to date have emphasized treatment of underlying interpersonal or dynamic issues with the hope that altering this psychopathology will improve the eating behavior (18, 19). Other therapeutic approaches address the behavior itself, placing emphasis on reducing unhealthy cognitions related to the eating behavior or providing specific behavioral techniques to reduce the symptoms and supply alternatives (20, 21). Often, group treatments have included all three approaches: psychodynamic, cognitive-behavioral, and behavioral.

The amount of structure built into the group is also an important issue. Stevens and Salisbury believe that the habitual nature of the behavior and the low self-esteem of bulimic patients make structure and direction essential early in treatment (18). Structure may also be increased by having more frequent sessions early in treatment to support interruption of the behavior (20, 21). Such considerations relate closely to a major treatment issue—that is, the therapist's expectation for interruption of the bulimic behaviors. Positions which have been advocated include the expectation of immediate cessation of the behavior after a period of behavioral self-monitoring (20), a contract for gradual elimination of the behavior (17), and a contract for reduction of the behavior to a level acceptable to the client (13, 21).

The effects of various optional group therapy procedures on the progress of bulimic patients are as yet inadequately evaluated. For example, the amount and content of patient contact outside the group for mutual support is one of the treatment questions at issue. Only two published group studies encouraged outside contact (20, 21). Whether the group should be closed or open and whether the number of therapeutic sessions should be fixed or variable also needs further evaluation. Although the use of male and female co-therapists has been considered optimal for group therapy in general (22), some group programs have elected to use one therapist to reduce the cost of treatment. Such issues as the sex of the therapists, the number of therapists, and whether or not a therapist who has experienced an eating disorder is more effective all need careful evaluation.

Group therapy may be used in different ways in the treatment of bulimia. Group psychotherapy has been proposed by many authors as the primary treatment for the interruption of bulimic behaviors (13, 18–21, 23, 24). In addition, brief group therapy has been used to interrupt the habitual daily cycle of bingeing and vomiting prior to insight-oriented therapy (25), as a way to stabilize behavior following either group therapy (20) or individual therapy (26) designed to interrupt the bulimic behavior, or in combination with other therapies (17). Finally, many different types of support groups for bulimic patients have been developed as a result of the high demand for treatment (27).

In the remainder of this paper, group therapy as the primary treatment of bulimia and the outcome of group studies to date will be reviewed. Discussion will focus on some principles of group treatment which may be important in the overall reduction of bulimic behaviors, and the importance of group therapy as a part of a comprehensive treatment system for eating disorders.

CHARACTERISTICS OF GROUPS REPORTED AS A PRIMARY TREATMENT FOR BULIMIA

We wish to emphasize that none of the groups described in the published studies were conducted as part of a rigorous research protocol. The therapeutic approaches demonstrated by treatments reported to date were often developed over time on the basis of therapist experiences and patient feedback (19–21). While none of the group studies reported using a single therapeutic approach, all of them reported using behavioral approaches to reduce the frequency of bulimic behaviors. All used female therapists, two with male co-therapists (19, 23). General characteristics of these groups are summarized in Table 1.

Boskind-Lodahl and White (13) first reported on the use of group therapy for bulimia in a program designed to treat females with "bulimarexia" who responded to a newspaper advertisement. Inclusion criteria for the group included the presence of binge-eating, self-induced vomiting or laxative abuse, marked concern over being fat, and low self-esteem (including fear of men and

Table 1. Clinical Characteristics of Group Treatments for Bulimia

Study	Theoretical Framework[a]	Goals	Format	Therapists
Boskind-Lodahl and White (13)	Experiential–behavioral	Increase self-esteem and satisfaction with feminine role	Closed, semistructured, 11 two-hour sessions with one six-hour marathon	Two female
White and Boskind-White (23)	Experiential–behavioral	Established by goal contracting	Closed, both structured and unstructured sessions, one week duration, two sessions daily (five hours) × five days	One female Male/female
Dixon and Kiecolt-Glaser (24)	Dynamic–behavioral	Reduce bulimic behavior	Open, unstructured, 10 weeks minimum, 1½ hours weekly	Two female
Johnson et al. (21)	Psychoeducational	Reduce bulimic behavior	Closed, structured, 12 two-hour sessions over nine weeks, socialization outside group encouraged	Two female
Stevens and Salisbury (18)	Dynamic–behavioral	Regular meals; weight stabilization; "free days"[b]; relating to others	Closed, decreasing structure, 16 weekly 1½-hour sessions minimum with one five-hour session	Female
Roy-Byrne et al. (19)	Psychodynamic–behavioral–supportive	One year group attendance; keeping food diary; understand illness	Open until filled, unstructured, weekly sessions for one year	Male/female
Mitchell et al. (20)	Behavioral; cognitive-behavioral	Group cessation of bulimia behavior; behavior stabilization	Closed, structured, two months duration, 18 sessions, decreasing in length (three hours to 1½ hours) and frequency (daily to weekly), socialization outside of group encouraged	One female[c]

[a] Reported by authors.
[b] No bulimic behaviors during the "free day."
[c] Multiple staff members (male and female) provided didactic portion of group.

distrust of women). The group treatment emphasized gestalt and behavioral techniques to increase awareness of the behavior and increase the group members' responsibility for their own actions. In addition, the group focused on the development of a healthy feminist perspective. The expectation for the group members was that they would set goals which would lead to increased self-esteem, with a subsequent decrease in the bulimic behavior. Goal contracting, role playing, assertiveness training, and a "feelings journal" for self-monitoring were employed as behavioral techniques.

White and Boskind-White (23) also treated patients who responded to a magazine article on bulimia with a brief, intensive, structured approach combining behavioral techniques with discussion of the underlying feminist issues described above (13). Specific techniques described were goal contracting, role playing, and group confrontation of members who failed to change their behavior. A female therapist conducted a morning group, and male and female co-therapists an afternoon group.

Dixon and Kiecolt-Glaser (24) provided another early description of an open group approach, which was complicated by a high dropout rate. The group was unstructured, with the primary behavioral techniques consisting of food diaries, goal setting, and education about behavioral chains and alternatives to binge-eating behavior.

More recently, Johnson et al. (21) described a group that met in 12 sessions over a period of nine weeks, with a highly structured, psychoeducational focus. Techniques to reduce unhealthy cognitions were included. Program elements valued by group members at follow-up were homework, short-term goal setting, behavioral self-monitoring, challenging assumptions about food and weight, and the strong emphasis on group support outside the therapy system. The group also provided assertiveness training and relaxation training, which were reported by the group members to be less valuable than other treatment techniques. The group was planned in phases, with the first four sessions emphasizing education about bulimia and behavioral self-monitoring, the next two sessions goal contracting, and the final six sessions assertiveness training, relaxation training, and other techniques to improve coping skills.

Roy-Byrne et al. (19) described a weekly, one-year pilot group combining a psychodynamic interpersonal approach with general support, plus behavioral and cognitive techniques. Members were accepted until the group contained an optimal number of participants. There were no specific expectations for reducing the symptomatic behavior. Patients in the group also participated in individual therapy, and some received pharmacotherapy during the course of the group. While the group was not structured or phased, the authors provide an excellent description of the sequence of symptoms that are presented by group members during the course of group therapy.

Stevens and Salisbury (18) described a dynamic–behavioral group which accepted group members who were living independently, were over 20 years of age, and had had no psychiatric hospitalizations for eating disorders. Although posttreatment measures were taken after 16 weeks, members were allowed to stay in the group and continue to participate through the 10-month follow-up. The group not only emphasized dynamic issues and behavioral principles of treatment but also dealt with unhealthy cognitions during the course of treatment. The authors reported that structure and staff control were necessary to provide sufficient support to interrupt the behavior. They described two phases in treatment, the first four to six sessions being devoted to behavioral prescriptions and the remainder of the 16 sessions to personal competence and relationship to others. Specific techniques included a food journal, contracting to eat three meals a day at least twice weekly, and emphasis on weight stabilization. During the second phase of treatment, "free days" with no bulimic behavior were suggested. At the time that the group was emphasizing intimacy and relating to others, a five-hour session was included. Most patients in the study were still in group therapy at the time of treatment follow-up at 10 months.

The University of Minnesota Program (20) reported on a two-month group approach that was primarily behavioral, with lesser emphasis on eliminating unhealthy cognitions and confronting feminist issues. There were staff expectations for the immediate cessation of the bulimic behavior after a period of self-monitoring and confirmation of the desire to stop the behavior. The group met with decreasing frequency over a two-month period, from three hours daily five days a week during the first week, to 1½ hours weekly by the second month. The three-hour sessions combined didactic discussion, group meals, and group therapy. The use of group meals in the middle of the three-hour group session introduced exposure to food and prevention of the vomiting response. The first three weeks were intended to complete interruption of the behavior and the last five weeks to stabilize the behavior. The educational components of the program were presented by either a male or a female thrapist with extensive knowledge about bulimia and the 1½-hour group sessions by a female therapist also knowledgeable about bulimia. The group effort was supported by individual sessions at pretreatment (prior to self-monitoring) and during the fourth and eighth weeks. Sessions to enlist support of friends and family were held the second and fourth weeks.

These pilot group experiences demonstrate the natural evolution of a multifaceted approach to group treatments of bulimia using a combination of behavioral and dynamic approaches. Further, group studies have emphasized a high level of structure early in treatment and suggest that treatment techniques may be more effective if applied sequentially. These techniques will be discussed in more detail in the final section of this chapter.

OUTCOME FOR GROUP THERAPIES USED AS A PRIMARY TREATMENT FOR BULIMIA

Any discussion on outcome of therapy must include selection and measurement of variables and criteria used to define satisfactory treatment outcome. The recording of the efficacy of group treatment in reducing the target behaviors of binge-eating and vomiting in bulimic patients, both at posttreatment and at follow-up, is essential. Additionally, improvements in social functioning, mood, weight stability, and eating behaviors are important treatment outcomes that should also be addressed. Recent studies (18, 21) have reported the frequency of the target behaviors (binge-eating and self-induced vomiting) at posttreatment and at follow-up. In addition, some researchers are advocating the use of binge-free time and binge-free days as important outcome variables (21). The time of measurement of variables also is of interest because of the fluctuating nature of bulimic behavior in relation to environmental pressures or stress. These fluctuations make even pretreatment baseline measures of questionable value. One method of compensating for this is to compare the month of highest binge-eating and vomiting frequency prior to treatment and the pretreatment baseline with the month of highest frequency during the follow-up period (36).

The definition of successful outcome for group therapy is another problem of major importance. While researchers in pharmacological treatments for bulimia have accepted a percentage change in symptoms as an outcome measure, attaining a reduction in frequency of bulimic behaviors to a predefined level or reaching a symptom-free state may be more appropriate outcome measures.

Evaluation of treatment outcome at follow-up entails two additional problems: the confounding effect of the lack of a clear-cut ending to treatment, and the method of gathering data. At least one group study (18) reports that subjects remained in the group during the entire follow-up period. However, this practice is very similar to psychopharmacologic studies with antidepressants (28), where the treatment is continued from the posttreatment evaluation to the follow-up evaluation. Similarly, group programs which have a clear-cut ending (20) may encourage patients to participate in weekly group therapy during the post-group follow-up.

Options available for collecting data at follow-up include self-report questionnaires and semi-structured or structured face-to-face or telephone interviews. The best comparison available of the two methods of outcome assessment for bulimia treatment comes from the study of Abraham et al. (29), which compared patient self-reports and face-to-face interviews as procedures for evaluating improvement during treatment. They reported that patients were much more critical as raters, counting mild over-eating as binge-eating, prescribed laxatives as laxative abuse, and small weight changes as weight instability. This finding would suggest that direct contact, which would permit some interpretation of patient responses, is preferable to self-report questionnaires.

Thus far, no published reports on group psychotherapy have used a rigorous research design. None of the groups used random assignment of patients to the treatment condition. Two early group studies which reported use of a control group (13, 24) did not follow the usual procedure of random assignment. In addition, most of the group treatment studies have used multiple therapeutic approaches, which makes evaluation of any particular treatment framework impossible. Consequently, none of the additional procedures for group therapy research were followed, such as monitoring and rating the therapy sessions to ensure that the therapeutic approach intended was actually conducted. Further, none of the group studies of which we are aware have excluded subjects who were in other forms of treatment, either individual psychotherapy or psychopharmacologic therapy. One study (19) reported that all the remaining group members at the end of the study were also engaged in individual therapy, and a substantial number were receiving antidepressant treatment. Finally, any calculations regarding outcome results should include treatment dropouts. Outcome of group studies to date is reported in Table 2 (posttreatment) and in Table 3 (follow-up). Outcome percentages include treatment dropouts and are based on reduction in bulimic behaviors to a specific level.

Posttreatment outcome results support the use of frequent sessions and extensive structure to interrupt the bulimic behavior (20). While the latter results were not maintained at follow-up, the outcome results of some weekly group approaches improved between posttreatment and follow-up (18, 24). The impact of a dynamic approach (dealing with underlying issues and unhealthy cognitions) on results at follow-up is demonstrated by the study by Stevens and Salisbury (18) of patients having no previous inpatient care for eating disorders. The fact that the group continued between posttreatment and follow-up evaluations does not diminish

Table 2. Posttreatment Outcome for Group Therapies for Bulimia

Study	Control	Started treatment	Treatment dropouts	Completed treatment	Markedly improved[b]	Remission[c]	Treatment[d] success
				Posttreatment Results n (%n)[a]			
Boskind-Lodahl and White (13)	Waiting list	13 (100)	1 (8)	12 (92)	?	4 (31)	?
Dixon and Kiecolt-Glaser (24)	Individual and waiting list	36 (100)	25 (69)	11 (31)	0 (0)	3 (8)	3 (8)
Johnson et al. (21)	None	13 (100)	3 (23)	10 (77)	2 (15)	2 (15)	4 (31)
Stevens and Salisbury (18)	None	8 (100)	2 (25)	6 (75)	3 (37)	0 (0)	3 (37)
Roy-Byrne et al. (19)	None	19 (100)	10 (53)	9 (47)	0 (0)	3 (16)	3 (16)
Mitchell et al. (20)	None	104 (100)	17 (16)	87 (84)	26 (25)[e]	49 (47)[e]	75 (72)[e]

[a] All percentages based on number of patients starting treatment.
[b] Markedly improved—all bulimic behaviors occur weekly or less (except reference 20).
[c] Remission—all bulimic behaviors occur monthly or less (except reference 20).
[d] Treatment success—markedly improved plus remission.
[e] Data from entire two-month treatment period: markedly improved—1—3 episodes of bulimic behavior; remission—no episodes of bulimic behavior.

Table 3. Outcome at Follow-up for Group Therapies for Bulimia

Study	Started treatment	Completed treatment	Time of follow-up	Follow-up Results n (%n)[a]				
				Lost to follow-up	Completed follow-up	Markedly[b] improved	Remission[c]	Treatment[d] success
Dixon and Kiecolt-Glaser (24)	36 (100)	11 (31)	nine–12 months	0 (0)	11 (31)	0 (0)	5 (14)	5 (14)
White and Boskind-White (23)	14 (100)	14 (100)	Informal six-month	0 (0)	14 (100)	?	3 (21)	?
Johnson et al. (21)	13 (100)	10 (77)	Six-month	0 (0)	10 (77)	0 (0)	1 (8)	1 (8)
Stevens and Salisbury (18)	8 (100)	6 (75)	Six-month	0 (0)	6 (75)	0 (0)	5 (62)	5 (62)
Mitchell et al. (36)	44 (100)	40 (91)	12–15 months	0 (0)	40 (91)	8 (18)[e]	17 (39)[e]	25 (57)[e]

[a] All percentages based on number of patients starting treatment.
[b] Markedly improved—all bulimic behaviors occur weekly or less.
[c] Remission—all bulimic behaviors occur monthly or less.
[d] Treatment success—markedly improved plus remission.
[e] Data reported as highest frequency for *any* four-week period during follow-up.

the importance of the positive outcome as much as it supports the use of continuing group therapy after the behavior is interrupted in order to stabilize healthy behaviors. Groups which have remained open to new members (19, 24) report higher dropout rates than closed groups. Since most of the therapists in groups reported to date have been females, there are no data to help assess the impact of the number and sex of therapists on treatment outcome.

While group psychotherapy has received increasing attention as a treatment for bulimia, the efficacy of combined individual and group therapy (17) and antidepressant therapies (30) has been demonstrated by controlled studies. The favorable treatment outcome reported by pilot studies of group psychotherapy for bulimia also requires confirmation by controlled studies.

Table 4. Outcome at Follow-up for Patients Who Completed Bulimia Treatment Programs, by Percent and (Percent Range)

Kind of Treatment	n	Markedly Improved[d]	Remission[d]	Treatment Success[d]
Group therapy (four studies) (18, 21, 24, 36)	67	12% (0–18)	42% (8–62)	54% (8–62)
Combined individual and group therapy (17)	30	27%	67%	93%
Individual psychotherapy (28)[a]	43	(17–31%)	(29–40%)	(46–71%)
Individual cognitive-behavioral (14)	11	9%	63%	72%
Individual behavioral (32)	5	0%	40%	40%
Antidepressants (tricyclic and MAOI only) (30)[b]	19	?	47%	?
Antidepressants (MAOI only) (33)[c]	10	0%	60%	60%

[a] Most were still in treatment at follow-up. Percentages do not include subjects lost to follow-up. Ranges include results from both self-report and interview.
[b] Based on 19 of 22 subjects originally on medication two months. Maintenance medication continued, but two subjects in remission without medication (personal communication, H. G. Pope, Jr.); 47% in complete remission.
[c] Based on 10 of 12 completing treatment; five of six remain on medication.
[d] As defined in Tables 2, 3.

Table 4 provides a comparison between group therapies and other therapeutic approaches for bulimia based on the number of persons who successfully completed treatment. Considering early pessimism about treatment results (31), it is satisfying to note the high percentage of positive response to current treatments. The four studies on group therapy that reported outcome at follow-up in terms of similar criteria have been combined (18, 21, 24, 36). The table also includes Lacey's combined individual and group therapy (17); a study of individual supportive psychotherapy (29); an example of individual cognitive behavioral therapy (14); and five cases of individual behavioral therapy using exposure and response prevention (32). The latter study was selected because most studies involving individual behavioral therapies are single case reports while this study uses the same design on multiple patients. These recent treatment results for exposure and response prevention are less encouraging than earlier studies with only two of the five patients symptom-free at follow-up. The comparison study for antidepressant therapy using either tricyclic or MAOI antidepressants included 19 of 22 subjects who completed at least two months of antidepressant treatment (30). Most had been treated sequentially with antidepressants to attain successful outcome. Many were being maintained on MAOIs. All but two subjects remained on medication at the time of follow-up, which was conducted for as long as two years after the initial treatment (personal communication, HG Pope Jr). The open study of Stewart et al. (33), involving 12 subjects, 10 of whom completed treatment, was selected as an example of outcome with MAO inhibitors.

The high treatment success of combined individual and group therapy (17) compares favorably with that of Fairburn's individual cognitive behavioral approach (14) and results with MAOIs (33). The 54 percent treatment success rate for group therapy is impressive considering the large number of groups, the wide range of outcome, and the different techniques used. Antidepressants, particularly MAO inhibitors, still demonstrate a high rate of remission from bulimic symptoms and constitute an important treatment modality for depressed bulimic patients.

The favorable outcome of initial pilot studies of group therapies for bulimia supports further evaluation with more rigorous research designs; however, results to date are sufficiently encouraging to continue use of group therapy as a major treatment modality for bulimia. With this in mind, we will review in the following section treatment techniques which many of the group programs seem to have developed in common on the basis of therapists' experience and patient feedback.

SOME PRINCIPLES OF GROUP TREATMENT FOR BULIMIA

In our discussion of treatment principles we will rely on clinical impressions derived from our own experience in providing group treatment for bulimic patients and on previously published reports. Undoubtedly, over time, many of these preliminary clinical impressions will be altered as research begins to evaluate the efficacy of individual components of groups.

Several stages must be considered in the treatment of bulimia: 1) evaluation and medical management, 2) interruption of the habitual daily pattern of bulimic behavior, 3) reduction of sporadic bulimic behavior in response to environmental stresses, and 4) stabilization of healthy eating behaviors. Before proceeding to the treatment principles which may have relevance to group treatment of bulimia, we will explore the role of evaluation and medical management as part of treatment.

Problems such as medical instability, laxative abuse, and depression, with the associated potential for suicide, should be assessed carefully at the time of the initial evaluation and be monitored throughout treatment. It is also desirable to educate the potential patient regarding the diagnosis, course, and treatment of bulimia and to involve the patient in the selection of appropriate treatment. For persons who have a sporadic pattern of bulimic behavior and are motivated for treatment, a weekly behavioral or cognitive behavioral group will often suffice, while a much more structured, intensive approach may be required for patients with daily binge-eating episodes. Patient motivation to enter treatment may be positively influenced if the evaluator has specific knowledge and experience regarding the treatment of eating disorders—in contrast, for example, to psychodynamic or behavioral therapists with less specialized skills.

Several additional program elements may be of value between evaluation and treatment. Behavioral self-monitoring, emphasized by Fairburn (14), may be used to reduce denial of the problem and further support the decision to engage in treatment. The use of a meal-planning clinic prior to group therapy provides dietary information to support the healthy eating behaviors necessary for successful treatment. An interim or preparatory group is a valuable support for bulimic patients who have a sense of desperation when asking for treatment. Motivation may be temporary, and these patients may be lost to treatment if immediate support is not available until the prescribed individual or group therapy is initiated. In addition to temporary support, an interim group can provide further education about bulimia, instruction regarding alternatives to binge-eating, and exercises to reinforce motivation for treatment. These interim support groups must be open and flexible in format. In addition, a suitable inpatient unit, specializing in eating disorder treatment, should be available for those for whom outpatient care is contraindicated. Our discussion of group treatment of bulimia will include potential problems during a particular treatment phase, treatment issues relating to that phase, elements of patient education, and specific treatment techniques.

Interruption of the Habitual Daily Pattern of Bulimic Behavior

We believe that in order to interrupt the habitual daily pattern of bulimic behavior, group therapy must be intensive—that is, the group should meet twice or more weekly and be highly structured (20). Other authors have supported the need for an intensive approach for both individual therapy (14) and group therapy (23), and for extensive staff direction and treatment structure (18, 21). Alternatives to an intensive group approach may be valuable for some patients—for example, intensive individual cognitive behavioral therapy or less structured group cognitive behavioral therapy with a high emphasis on the group members' setting their own goals for reduction of the bulimic behavior.

Problems during the phase of interrupting the behavior fall into two general areas: 1) the habitual daily binge/purge pattern, which in some ways resembles that of chemical dependency, and 2) motivation. The majority of therapists now concur that some type of structured behavioral intervention is necessary to interrupt the daily binge/purge cycle. Motivation presents several problems: First, continuing the behavior offers some rewards. For example, dysphoric feelings are sometimes reduced during the binge/purge process (34, 35), and self-induced vomiting has been reported as a relaxing and reinforcing behavior (15, 34). Second, motivation is decreased by fear of failure, which is often realistic, as bulimics have frequently experienced multiple treatment failures. Fin. attempts to stop bulimic behavior are often associated with en. tional lability and dysphoric symptoms (17). Without a clear u. derstanding of such symptoms, stopping the behavior may become exceedingly stressful.

Prior to interruption of the behaviors, patients may benefit from behavioral self-monitoring, such as recording planned meals versus actual food consumption; reasons for deviating from the planned eating behavior; and the feelings associated with the unplanned eating behavior. This technique has been applied to successful individual (14) and combined individual and group programs (17) and is recommended during the early phases of treatment. Prior to interrupting the behavior it is also helpful to have patients record the advantages and disadvantages of continuing the behavior. For most patients, such an inventory will help reinforce the decision to stop the behavior. Patient education during this phase should also include further information about the course and treatment of bulimia so that the patients may confidently challenge previously held myths about the illness (3).

As patients begin the interruption phase, the group becomes a powerful tool in providing support and structure. During this time mutual support by group members outside the group is most valuable, through direct support during difficult periods, sharing activities, or regular phone contacts. Behavioral techniques, which may also be of value during this phase of treatment, are stimulus control or avoidance (including interruption of behavioral cues and chains), exposure and response prevention, and reinforcement of desired behavior by both group members and therapists. For example, group members who continue to binge-eat may be encouraged by the group to develop a plan, either on their own or with the aid of group suggestions, which will allow them to eliminate the eating behaviors that they no longer desire, rather than dwelling on failure. It is equally important that patients plan in advance and then consume three nutritious meals daily to assure that their food intake will maintain their weight during treatment.

Reduction of Sporadic Bulimic Behavior in Response to Environmental Stresses

After the daily binge/purge cycle is interrupted and the bulimic behavior ceases or becomes sporadic, treatment emphasis changes. New problems include binge-eating or the desire to binge-eat in response to various environmental stresses; the dysphoria associated with treatment (17); and the maintainance of adequate food intake.

Treatment during this phase concentrates on the new problem of isolating and defining binge situations. During this period of relative instability, it may be desirable for patients to avoid environmental stimulants to binge-eating, including specific foods, situations, and certain family interactions. At this time, group members begin to define, confront, and alter unhealthy cognitions involving eating and begin to practice skills designed to reduce stress or promote the ability to cope with stress.

Since most bulimic patients have distorted ideas about the number of calories required to maintain weight (3), special attention must be given to repetition of earlier education on nutrition. Discussion of the sequence and course of dysphoric symptoms associated with treatment is also beneficial. Patient education about cognitive behavioral techniques, stress management, anxiety reduction, assertiveness, and dealing with family interactions is important in combatting the problems of this phase of treatment.

Stabilization of Healthy Eating Behaviors

During the period of behavioral stabilization, it may be valuable to offer one or more weekly groups to teach problem-solving techniques, to continue work with relapse prevention, and to help patients develop a more flexible lifestyle. Ancillary services that may be of value during the period of behavior stabilization are family or couples therapy, individual psychotherapy, programs for assertiveness training, and training in stress management.

Problems which arise during this treatment phase may include continuation of many dysphoric symptoms, including grief from loss of the behavior, boredom from having additional free time, and depression. Another problem during this period is the development of very rigid, inflexible lifestyles and eating habits for fear that the behavior will recur if the daily routine is altered.

Major treatment issues during this phase include the method of exposure to feared situations and foods, and antidepressive treatment. While most clinicians agree that a gradual, supported, controlled exposure to feared foods and situations is necessary to develop the flexibility needed to prevent relapse, some advocate that the patient engage in binge-eating behavior to demonstrate that an isolated episode of binge-eating can occur and then be brought under control with no further episodes. Most therapists would also agree that persistent symptoms of depression following cessation of the bulimic behavior are an indication for antidepressant treatment.

Treatment considerations often include work with unhealthy cognitions associated with problems that do not involve food. Relapse prevention may also be emphasized, with each group member consolidating her own repertoire of coping techniques, developing a plan for exposure to feared foods and feared situations, and defining the support network and after-care plan which is appropriate for her. Potential elements of the after-care system may include dynamic psychotherapy, eating-disorder self-help groups, doing volunteer work with people with eating disorders, or participating in women's awareness groups. One approach to completion of the stabilization phase is the development of a specific relapse plan, which is typed, memorized, and carried by the group members. The stabilization phase should also accomplish a gradual reduction of group supports as self-esteem and confidence increase.

We have reviewed the limited information available from published studies on bulimia and discussed techniques that we believe are of value in group treatment. We have also argued in this paper for a treatment structure for bulimia which has as the major focus outpatient group psychotherapy appropriately delivered. We believe that such an outpatient approach, carefully monitored by medical team members, offers effective treatment for bulimia when used alone or in appropriate combination with individual or pharmacologic treatments.

References

1. Mitchell JE, Pyle RL: The bulimic syndrome in normal weight individuals: a review. International Journal of Eating Disorders 1:61–73, 1982

2. Mitchell JE: Medical complications of anorexia nervosa and bulimia. Psychiatr Med 1:229–255, 1984

3. Fairburn CG: Binge-eating and its management. Br J Psychiatry 141:631–633, 1982

4. Fairburn CG, Cooper PJ: Self-induced vomiting and bulimia nervosa: an undetected problem. Br Med J 284:1153–1155, 1982

5. Stangler RS, Printz AM: DSM-III: psychiatric diagnoses in a university population. Am J Psychiatry 137:937–940, 1980

6. Halmi KA, Falk JR, Schwartz E: Binge-eating and vomiting: a survey of a college population. Psychol Med 11:697–706, 1981

7. Cooper PJ, Fairburn CG: Binge-eating and self-induced vomiting in the community, a preliminary study. Br J Psychiatry 142:139–144, 1983

8. Pope HG Jr, Hudson JI, Yurgelun-Todd D: Anorexia nervosa and bulimia among 300 suburban women shoppers. Am J Psychiatry 141:292–294, 1984

9. Agras WS, Barlow DH, Chapin HN, et al: Behavior modification of anorexia nervosa. Arch Gen Psychiatry 30:279–286, 1974

10. Wing RR, Jeffrey RW: Outpatient treatments of obesity: a comparison of methodology and clinical results. Int J Obesity 3:261–279, 1979

11. Penick SM, Hilton R, Fox S, et al: Behavior modification in the treatment of obesity. Psychosom Med 33:49–55, 1971

12. Hollon SD, Shaw BF: Group cognitive therapy for depressed patients, in Cognitive Therapy for Depression: A Treatment Manual. Edited by Beck AT, Rush AJ, Shaw BF, et al. New York, Guilford Press, 1979

13. Boskind-Lodahl M, White WC: The definition and treatment of bulimarexia in college women: a pilot study. Journal of the American College Health Association 27:84–86, 97, 1978

14. Fairburn C: A cognitive behavioral approach to the treatment of bulimia. Psychol Med 11:707–711, 1981

15. Rosen JC, Leitenberg H: Bulimia nervosa: treatment with exposure and response prevention. Behav Ther 13:117–124, 1982

16. Hoage CM, Gray JJ: Group behavior therapy with exposure and response prevention as a treatment for bulimia. Paper presented at First International Conference on Eating Disorders, New York, April 1984

17. Lacey JH: Bulimia nervosa, binge-eating, and psychogenic vomiting: a controlled treatment study and long-term outcome. Br Med J 286:1609–1613, 1983

18. Stevens EV, Salisbury JD: Group therapy for bulimic adults. Am J Orthopsychiatry 54:156–161, 1984

19. Roy-Byrne P, Lee-Benner K, Yager J: Group therapy for bulimia: a year's experience. International Journal of Eating Disorders 3:97–116, 1984

20. Mitchell JE, Hatsukami D, Goff G, et al: An intensive outpatient group treatment program for patients with bulimia, in A Handbook of Psychotherapy of Anorexia Nervosa and Bulimia. Edited by Garner D, Garfinkel P. New York, Guilford Press, 1984

21. Johnson C, Connors M, Stuckey M: Short-term group treatment of bulimia: a preliminary report. International Journal of Eating Disorders 2:199–208, 1983

22. Yalom ID: The Theory and Practice of Group Psychotherapy. New York, Basic Books, 1975

23. White WC, Boskind-White M: An experiential-behavioral approach to the treatment of bulimarexia. Psychotherapy: Theory, Research and Practice 18:501–507, 1981

24. Dixon KN, Kiecolt-Glaser J: An integrated group therapy approach to bulimia. Paper presented at the 134th Annual Meeting of the American Psychiatric Association, New Orleans, May 1981

25. Tanenbaum R, Berman M: Psychotherapies for bulimia: which course first? Paper presented at First International Conference on Eating Disorders, New York, April 1984

26. Doane HM: Famine at the Feast. Ann Arbor, Michigan, Eric Counseling and Personnel Services Clearinghouse, 1983

27. Enright AB, Butterfield P, Berkowitz B: Self-help and support groups in the management of eating disorders, in A Handbook of Psychotherapy of Anorexia Nervosa and Bulimia. Edited by Garner D, Garfinkel P. New York, Guilford Press, 1984

28. Walsh BT, Stewart JW, Roose SP, et al: Treatment of bulimia with phenelzine Arch Gen Psychiatry 41:1105–1109, 1984

29. Abraham SF, Mira M, Llewellyn-Jones D: Bulimia: a study of outcome. International Journal of Eating Disorders 2:175–180, 1984

30. Pope HG Jr, Hudson JI, Jonas JM, et al: Bulimia treated with imipramine: a placebo-controlled, double-blind study. Am J Psychiatry 140:554–558, 1983

31. Russell G: Bulimia nervosa: an ominous variant of anorexia nervosa. Psychol Med 9:429–448, 1979

32. Leitenberg H, Gross J, Peterson J, et al: Analysis of an anxiety model and the process of change during exposure plus response prevention treatment of bulimia nervosa. Behav Ther 15:3–20, 1984

33. Stewart JW, Walsh BT, Wright L, et al: An open trial of MAOI's in bulimia. J Clin Psychiatry 45:217–219, 1984

34. Johnson C, Larson R: Bulimia: an analysis of moods and behavior. Psychosom Med 44:341–351, 1982

35. Abraham SF, Beumont PJV: How patients describe bulimia or binge-eating. Psychol Med 12:625–635, 1982

36. Mitchell JE, Davis L, Goff G, et al: A follow-up study of patients with bulimia. International Journal of Eating Disorders, in press

6

Constructing an Inpatient Treatment Program for Bulimia

Harry E. Gwirtsman, M.D.
David T. George, M.D.
Walter H. Kaye, M.D.
Michael H. Ebert, M.D.

6

Constructing an Inpatient Treatment Program for Bulimia

Along with increasing awareness of the startling current prevalence of bulimia in the female population (1–3), physicians have realized that its complications are sometimes serious enough to require inpatient care. Before describing the inpatient treatment program that we have been developing, we shall briefly review the material in earlier chapters on characteristic symptoms and indicated treatment.

Studies of bulimia indicate a high coincidence with affective disorder and substance abuse, especially alcoholism (4, 5). Family studies have corroborated this finding, with four of five investigations demonstrating an unusually high prevalence of depression and alcoholism in first-degree relatives of bulimics (5–9). In three of these studies the investigators carried out interviews of the family. The fact that Strober's study (6) looked at underweight bulimics (bulimarectics) and Hudson's (7) studied normal weight bulimics does not appear to have altered the overall agreement among the findings. Axis II disorders have also been found to be associated with the bulimic syndrome, although this has not been as carefully studied (5, 8).

The medical complications in patients with bulimia, as mentioned in Chapter Three, by Dr. Halmi, can result in death due to cardiac arrhythmias or acute gastric dilatation (10), electrolyte abnormalities (11), irritation of the gastrointestinal tract, hypersecretion of amylase and hypertrophy of the salivary glands (12), dental problems (15), and disturbances of all endocrine axes studied including the hypothalamic-pituitary-adrenal (8, 13), -thyroid (8, 14), and -ovarian (4).

Bulimics are seen by pediatricians, gynecologists, internists, and psychiatric practitioners in outpatient settings for such problems as hypoglycemia, menstrual complaints, malaise and weakness, and depression. Inpatient help is sometimes necessary, either on an intensive care unit for treatment of cardiac arrhythmias or, more frequently, on a psychiatric unit. The most common reasons for psychiatric hospitalization are: 1) coexisting major depression with suicidal ideation or attempt; and 2) inability to function at work or school due to the disruptive effects of the habitual binge-eating and purging. Less frequently, bulimics are brought into the hospital either by concerned relatives or spouses who find the condition intolerable, or by law enforcement agencies following repeated episodes of shoplifting for food or laxatives. It is not unusual for a bulimic to be followed as an outpatient for somatic complaints without disclosing the bulimia to the treating physician. However, by the time bulimics require hospitalization, they have become unable to tolerate their symptoms and no longer hide them from concerned relatives and from practitioners.

CRITERIA FOR ADMISSION

Patients who fail with outpatient psychotherapy or pharmaco-therapy are candidates for inpatient management. The coexistence of a major depressive disorder which is either incapacitating or is accompanied by suicidal intent is a compelling indication for admission to a psychiatric unit.

Because the practice of purging may result in medical complications that may be life-threatening, therapists who follow outpatient bulimics should be alert to symptoms of fatigue, palpitations, lethargy, or confusion, which may be the result of electrolyte imbalance such as potassium and sodium depletion, and may produce cardiac disturbances. In general, vomiting is accompanied by acid-base disequilibrium into the basic range. Renal compensation for hydrogen ion loss causes wasting of the potassium ion, in a classical picture of hypokalemic alkalosis with a concurrent increase in the bicarbonate ion. Chloride ion is also frequently diminished in this profile, since it is purged as hydrogen chloride, the major acid in stomach secretions. Laxative abuse, especially if accompanied by ingestion of large amounts of water, causes the electrolyte abnormalities seen with chronic diarrhea, which include hyponatremia and hypochloremia. These electrolyte disturbances, if severe enough, may provoke cardiographic changes, including the appearance of U waves, ST and T wave changes, prolongation of QT and even QRS intervals, and tachyarrhythmias of the irritable or reentrant varieties. Periodic electrolyte checks and EKGs are necessary in monitoring patients who binge and purge frequently.

Clinicians should also consider disability due to bulimia as a possible criterion for admission. Severely affected patients may binge and purge so frequently that they begin to commit significant proportions of their waking time and financial resources to that behavior. When this occurs, it is often accompanied by serious declines in work or school performance or inadequate participation in family activities. Another consequence of frequent binge-purge cycles is the inability of an outpatient physician to conduct a reasonable medication trial. These types of disabling outcomes, and especially the compromise of child care with bulimic mothers, may benefit from hospitalization which brings the behaviors under control.

RELEVANCE OF OUTPATIENT TREATMENT LITERATURE

Treatment of bulimic behavior patterns has most frequently been studied in the outpatient setting, as described in detail in Chapters Four and Five. For example, four recent studies involving small samples of bulimics (16–19) and four case studies (20–23) employing group and individual treatment approaches have used several therapy paradigms, but usually advocate the behavioral and cognitive methods in the initial phase of the programs. The total number of patients polled from all studies is small (until recently, well under 100), and adequate controls were included in only one-half of the studies. In general, brief psychotherapy appears to be quite effective, with 70–90 percent of the patients reporting at least a moderate improvement in their symptomatology, and 30–80 percent reporting themselves to be binge-free. Self-reports are always open to question, but as yet there are no independent methods of confirming that bingeing and purging has ceased. Several studies provide some short-term follow-up data for up to one year after completion of the program. These follow-up results are not quite as encouraging and indicate a recidivist rate of 15–30 percent, though 45–71 percent of respondents were still binge free at the time of follow-up (17–19).

With respect to the role of pharmacotherapy as an adjunct to psychotherapy (see Chapters Four and Seven), significant anti-bulimic activity has been demonstrated for tricyclic antidepressants, monoamine oxidase inhibitors, lithium carbonate, and diphenylhydantoin (24–27).

Clinicians who have experience with bulimic patients recognize that the disorder is not monolithic but has a broad spectrum of psychopathology, with varying degrees of severity. The outpatient samples in most of the psychotherapy and pharmacotherapy studies demonstrated these characteristics.

Since the programs cited above only rarely treated inpatients, it might be argued that the results achieved may not be applicable to an inpatient subpopulation. Outcome studies with inpatient bulimics are a research priority, but in constructing an inpatient treatment program, one must of course consider the possible implications of the outpatient studies.

USE OF PSYCHIATRIC MODELS IN THE INPATIENT TREATMENT OF BULIMIC SYMPTOMS

Because bulimia in normal weight persons is a recently defined syndrome in the modern psychiatric lexicon, there are relatively few models to guide research or treatment strategies. This discussion, which is based on our clinical experiences in the context of a research program on the psychobiology of bulimia at the National Institute of Mental Health, will propose several models that may aid in an understanding of the syndrome, and then will use these models in constructing an inpatient treatment plan.

Addiction Model

In attempting to understand bulimic behavior, perhaps the most obvious model is that of addiction. Theoretically, addiction can be understood in the context of a stimulus and response paradigm. In bulimia, anxiety is often present, related to the question of whether or not to binge-eat, and food relieves such anxiety. Clinically, bulimics appear to share many of the symptoms characteristic of substance-dependent individuals. They engage in repetitive, stereotyped behaviors involving ingestion of food and purging. Often these behaviors follow a progressively intensified course, increasing in frequency and severity with continued repetition. Bulimics find it extremely difficult to cease such behavior on their own, and show severe anxiety and irritability if they are prevented from binge-eating or purging. Episodes are likely to be elaborately planned and carried out, and frequently become very disruptive, leading to the exclusion of other important daily activities. Food acquisition may become a driving, compelling force, even leading to larcenous behavior similar to that seen with narcotic addictions.

Additional support for the addiction model comes from family studies, which point to a probable genetic overlap between bulimia and alcohol abuse, and physiologic data are emerging (see Chapter Two) which suggest that binge-eating and vomiting may be more closely related to biological malfunction than to an underlying psychiatric diathesis. In other words, the physiological or psychological changes either caused by or relieved by bulimic behavior may be self-perpetuating. If so, the addiction model would usefully explain many of the phenomena observed in bulimic patients and would suggest that treatment should focus upon abstinence from binge-eating and purging as a primary goal.

Cultural Model

Cultural factors are often important in influencing norms of attractiveness, and currently, the ideal of sexual attractiveness that is being popularized in the media is exemplified by progressively thinner female models. This process defines obesity as sexually unattractive and creates fears—often unwarranted—in individuals with self-image problems. Bulimics who do not purge may eventually develop profound obesity, whereas purging bulimics often engage in the behavior in order to avoid becoming overweight. Data from our normal weight bulimic group suggest that their caloric intake is significantly lower than that in our normal controls. If this finding is replicable, we would speculate that purging might act as an effective weight control device in patients who are afraid of exceeding culturally mandated weight limits, but whose physiology is so inefficient that mere dieting would not be sufficient to create the desired weight loss. In other words, some normal weight bulimics may be able to sustain a culturally defined "attractive" weight only by engaging in purging. Indeed, many report that the purging actually preceded the binge-eating. An obesity model of bulimia suggests that health care professionals must take seriously the role that body image disturbance plays in this disorder, and must develop a carefully planned program to achieve metabolic balance, including monitored caloric intake and aerobic exercise.

Personality Disorder Model

Bulimics also display several characteristics which are observed in Axis II disorders. Anger is a frequent problem, whether suppressed or expressed, and may be the source of either impulsive acting out or, when turned inward, the development of depression and labile mood swings. Usually, there are underlying problems with social relationships, characterized more by turmoil and inability to form mature interpersonal bonds. Difficulties with self-esteem contribute to this, as well as persistent conflicts related to issues of individuation and separation. Avoidance behavior associated with a broad constellation of anxieties and phobic patterns may be seen. In the treatment setting, bulimics with such personality problems may be observed to rely heavily upon more primitive defense mechanisms such as splitting, projection, and denial. To the extent that this occurs, the treatment program must have internal consistency, must supply constant cross-validation of reality by staff members, and must provide support while simultaneously seeking to avoid enmeshment of staff in patient's problems and needs. Brief, intense hospital exposure followed by a more prolonged transition to outpatient treatment may be very therapeutic to bulimics with personality disorders.

Somatic Model

In illnesses that are believed to have both psychiatric and somatic components often one finds an inability to express frustrations and conflictual feelings. Development of somatic or behavioral symptoms apparently is exacerbated as a consequence of such constriction. Bulimics appear to have such difficulties and tend to express many of their psychological conflicts somatically. Underlying the bulimic activity, one may find severe anxiety which is poorly expressed or understood, and which may often be relieved rapidly and reliably, albeit briefly, by binge-eating. Treatment programs should take into account the psychosomatic illness model and develop strategies for prompting bulimics to express their psychological problems through means other than behavioral acting out or through somatic symptom formation. This might be partially accomplished with an assertiveness training program. Additionally, anxiety reduction strategies should be put into effect throughout the treatment program so that the perceived need for bulimic symptoms is attenuated.

Depression Model

As we indicated early in this chapter, depressive features are common among bulimics, although only a small percentage appear to meet criteria for major affective disorder. Neuroendocrine data are also in line with this hypothesis, demonstrating a surprising coincidence both in dexamethasone suppression (DST) and thyrotropin-releasing hormone stimulation (TRH stimulation) abnormalities in small samples of bulimics and depressives (8, 28). Finally, recent investigations have demonstrated that pharmacologic dosages of antidepressant agents also have significant—and often profound—antibulimic effects (24–27), creating yet another area of biologic overlap in these two disorders. Depressive features may be secondary to bulimic behavior patterns, but treatment programs should not err by withholding treatment for depression while waiting for the eating disorder to improve. It remains unclear whether antidepressant medication should be used strictly to treat the eating disorder even if depressive signs and symptoms are not prominently exhibited.

INPATIENT TREATMENT PROGRAM

An inpatient treatment program taking into account the symptom complex of bulimia and the possible etiological factors within that complex, as hypothesized in the above models, has been developed and piloted by the authors at the National Institute of Mental Health. It can be conceptualized in three phases—the initial phase: abstinence; the intermediate phase: stress inoculation; and the termination phase: outpatient transition. Table 1 presents the outline for this program.

Initial Phase: Abstinence

The abstinence phase begins as soon as the patient arrives in the hospital. During this phase, the major goal is to interrupt the behavior of binge-eating and purging. An associated goal is to regularize meals and provide the patient with an adequate number of calories to maintain the admission weight.

These goals are accomplished by placing the patient under close staff supervision. This may involve a locked unit in which patients cannot have free access to food. Many unit restrictions pervade this phase of the program, including: locking of bathroom doors to prevent postprandial vomiting; room searches to find hidden food and laxatives; and removal of wastebaskets so that patients cannot vomit into them. Food is not available to patients except during specified mealtimes and designated snack times. During mealtimes patients are required to sit at the table and consume their meal under staff supervision. While in the bathroom, patients are observed so as to prevent them from purging either in the toilet or in the shower. Additionally, patients are told that staff will be responsible for monitoring their caloric intake. A registered dietitian should be part of the treatment team in order to deliver expert dietary counseling. Patients are placed on a diet that is presumed to be adequate for their nutritional needs, and urged to

Table 1.   Inpatient Treatment Program for Bulimia (Four to Six Weeks)

	Goals	Strategies
Initial phase: abstinence (one to two weeks)	1. Response prevention 2. Meal regularization 3. Staff monitoring of caloric intake	1. Close observation 2. Active social support 3. Unit restrictions 4. Food restriction except at mealtimes

Intermediate phase: stress inoculation (one to two weeks)	1. Stress inoculation (exposure in vivo)
	2. Weight maintenance
	3. Cognitive restructuring
		1. Relaxation of bathroom restrictions
		2. Short passes; low stress
		3. Group and individual psychotherapy; family therapy
		4. Eating disorders milieu
		5. Monitoring of surreptitious binge-eating or vomiting
		   a. Active surveillance
		   b. Amylase and electrolytes
		6. Aerobics program

Termination phase: outpatient transition (one to two weeks)	1. Transition to outpatient setting
	2. Weight maintenance off hospital diet
	3. Maintenance of abstinence
		1. Complete relaxation of bathroom restrictions
		2. Food preparation on the unit
		3. Longer passes (overnight)
		4. Surveillance and physiological monitoring
		5. Continuation and intensification of psychotherapy
		   a. Encouragement to express feelings
		   b. Allow patients to share difficulties concerning adherence
		   c. Problem-solving around life skills

eat all the food presented to them. This exposure to food stimuli characteristically generates a great deal of anxiety. Most bulimics often develop feelings of bloating, fullness, and constipation as soon as their purging is controlled, which results in the unrealistic expectation that retained food will cause rapid weight gain. Usually this can be handled with reassurance, but occasionally constipation must be treated with enemas or with bulk, nonabsorbable laxatives.

Psychotherapy begins with active social support and is designed to encourage patients to discuss the stress of abstinence with therapist and staff. Initially, patients feel relieved and even somewhat elated that their behavior is under control, but this is soon replaced by irritability, anxiety, and depression as abstinence progresses. These reactions often occur because the patient is suddenly deprived of an activity which had previously consumed enormous amounts of intense mental and physical energy, and may feel lost with all her (his) newly created "free time." When this happens, the patient may resort to lying and manipulation as the stress of abstinence builds. Other mechanisms of defense are somatizing and staff splitting. Active staff confrontation of food hoarding, surreptitious vomiting, and laxative abuse is essential in maintaining the atmosphere of control. Somatic complaints should be examined medically if warranted. Simultaneously, the staff should interpret to the patient that psychological stress can also produce these symptoms and that they must be dealt with psychologically as well as physically. Overall, it is important during this phase of treatment for involved staff to remain in frequent contact with one another so that everyone is aware of any changes made in the treatment plan.

Intermediate Phase: Stress Inoculation

The second phase of the treatment program begins within one to two weeks of admission. The major goal of this phase is for the patient and therapist to design a program of gradually relaxing restrictions and increasing activity, in a supportive environment. Associated aims include the maintenance of weight (for normal weight persons) or a readjustment of weight (anorectics), and cognitive restructuring of dysfunctional thoughts and attitudes.

During this phase, bulimics are educated cooperatively by physician and dietitian on their caloric needs and how best to provide them. A realistic weight goal is negotiated (usually the patient will request a weight target 10–15 percent below ideal body weight). The patient is then counseled to remain within two to four pounds or one to two kilograms of that weight target by varying her daily caloric intake. This allows the patient to begin to feel in control of her weight without needing to resort to bingeing and vomiting. The bathroom restrictions are relaxed in a gradual fashion, permitting the patient to be unobserved during designated periods that are temporally removed from mealtime—for example, before breakfast. Thus, even if purging is attempted, it will be ineffectual, since most or all of the previous meal will have passed the pylorus. Additionally, the patient and therapist begin to design a series of short passes oriented to the patient's level of apprehension. Initially, only "low stress" passes are permitted—for example, going for a walk or jog for half an hour, an accompanied pass to shop, and so forth. The treatment program should develop a method of monitoring abstinence compliance during passes. Patients are encouraged to reveal to staff their off-unit binges but, in general, this method of monitoring has been disappointingly uncertain. We have found, however, that serum amylase and electrolytes are very useful when obtained immediately after the patient has returned from pass. The carbon dioxide is usually elevated from baseline and remains high for several hours after vomiting. The amylase is more sensitive to binges and vomiting, but rises in amylase often do not return to normal for several days following a binge. Used together, these two measures are helpful to the clinician, allowing him to confront the patient realistically and leading to a more therapeutic outcome.

Because normal weight bulimics usually have an unrealistic fear of weight gain, they often have a covert desire to lose weight during the treatment program. Patients should be advised to remain within a given weight range and should be given increasing control of menu selection after the dietitian and physician have established the individual's daily caloric requirement. As activity increases, caloric requirements may rise moderately, and most patients will be gratified to find themselves consuming reasonably nutritious meals without increasing their weight. Some normal weight bulimics, however, will have diminished caloric requirements compared to their nonbulimic counterparts. Such patients should be confronted with this reality and counseled carefully concerning their dietary selections.

As restrictions begin to relax, the patient should be encouraged to begin an aerobic exercise program. Besides the usual benefits of such a program, it is particularly helpful in alleviating anxiety about the calories consumed that day. Every 10 minutes of intense aerobic activity expends approximately 100 kcals, and less intense activity (such as walking) expends approximately one-half that amount.

Termination Phase: Outpatient Transition

The final phase of the treatment program serves as a transition period that prepares the patient for discharge. Its goals include: weight maintenance off a hospital diet; maintenance of abstinence; and self-control while on very stressful passes.

During this phase, bathroom restrictions are further relaxed until the patient has free private access to bathrooms. Off-unit activities are extended to include overnight passes. Both patient and therapist collaborate to expose the patient to difficult situations, such as going to a party where there is particularly tempting food, going to a shopping mall alone, going to a restaurant with family, friends, and business associates. Although the patient has increased freedom, active surveillance and physiological monitoring are maintained, and patients are encouraged to discuss their passes candidly with staff.

By this point, the patient should be maintaining his or her weight on a hospital diet. For selected individuals, the transition phase might include a period of purchasing groceries and cooking meals on the ward in order to better approximate the conditions of a nonhospital setting.

Psychotherapy during this phase must be intensified, with fo-cus on the expression of frustrations and anger in an appropriate manner, the development of the therapist as an ally concerning food adherence difficulties, and effective problem-solving in social relationships and day-to-day issues.

Although antibulimic medication should be administered to patients early in the hospitalization if the patient has major depres-sive disorder or a history of bipolarity, for most patients the clini-cian might consider administering medication during the latter phases of hospitalization as a reinforcement measure. This might prevent the patient from attributing any early positive response to a medication effect rather than to the treatment program and her own efforts. Placing a patient on medications early in the hospital-ization also might make the patient less available for participation in the behavioral or cognitive psychotherapeutic aspects of the program, which may be very important in the maintenance of abstinence. Finally, for patients who fail at repeated attempts at psychotherapy, medication becomes an alternate approach. A full discussion of medication therapy will be found in the final chap-ter.

APPRAISAL

Although our pilot program involves some of the above recom-mendations, a complete inpatient program such as the one pro-posed has not yet been tested experimentally. Further research should examine in more detail various aspects of a total inpatient program in order to refine such treatment and establish its valid-ity. For example, one important issue is the approach taken toward bingeing and vomiting on the unit. How long should staff enforce abstinence from bingeing via direct surveillance? How can behav-ioral contracts be made more palatable to bulimics in an inpatient setting, allowing them to interpose more acceptable behaviors in place of their binges and purges? What role do dynamic psycho-therapy and pharmacotherapy play, and at what stage should they be introduced into the treatment program? There are currently no controlled outcome studies that pertain to these situations, and multiple case studies or single case reports do not suffice to establish the efficacy of a method of inpatient management. There is a great need for such investigations. As bulimic disorder is currently being treated by many public and private institutions, more specific guidelines are necessary for inpatient care managers and therapists alike, in order to optimize therapeutic outcome.

References

1. Halmi KA, Falk JR, Schwartz E: Binge-eating and vomiting: a survey of a college population. Psychol Med 11:697–706, 1981

2. Stangler RS, Printz AM: *DSM-III*: Psychiatric diagnosis in a university population. Am J Psychiatry 137:937–940, 1980

3. Hawkins RC, Clement PF: Development and construct validation of a self-report measure of binge-eating tendencies. Addict Behav 5:219–226, 1980

4. Russell G: Bulimia nervosa: an ominous variant of anorexia nervosa. Psychol Med 9:429–448, 1979

5. Pyle RL, Mitchell JE, Eckert ED: Bulimia: a report of 34 cases. J Clin Psychiatry 42:60–64, 1981

6. Strober M, Salkin B, Burroughs J, et al: Validity of the bulimia-restricter distinction in anorexia nervosa: parental personality characteristics and family psychiatric morbidity. J Nerv Ment Dis 170:345–351, 1982

7. Hudson JI, Pope HG, Jr, Jonas JM, et al: Family history study of anorexia nervosa and bulimia. Br J Psychiatry 142:133–138, 1983

8. Gwirtsman HE, Roy-Byrne P, Yager J, et al: Neuroendocrine abnormalities in bulimia. Am J Psychiatry 140:559–563, 1983

9. Stern SL, Dixon KN, Nemzer E, et al: Affective disorder in the families of women with normal weight bulimia. Am J Psychiatry 141:1224–1227, 1984

10. Mitchell JE, Pyle RL, Miner RA: Gastric dilatation as a complication of bulimia. Psychosomatics 23:96–98, 1982

11. Mitchell JE, Pyle RL, Eckert ED, et al: Electrolyte and other physiological abnormalities in patients with bulimia. Psychol Med 13:273–278, 1983

12. Levin PA, Falko JM, Dixon K, et al: Benign parotid enlargments in bulimia. Ann Intern Med 93:827–829, 1980

13. Hudson JI, Pope HG, Jr, Jonas JM, et al: Hypothalamic-pituitary adrenal axis hyperactivity in bulimia. Psychiatry Res 8:111–117, 1983

14. Mitchell JE, Bantle JP: Metabolic and endocrine investigations in women of normal weight with the bulimia syndrome. Biol Psychiatry 18:355–365, 1983

15. Friedman EJ, Stolar M, Kramer MR, et al: Psychological and endocrine evaluation of bulimia. Paper presented at the 137th Annual Meeting of the American Psychiatric Association, Los Angeles, May 1984

16. Boskind-Lodahl M, White WC: The definition and treatment of bulimarexia in college women: a pilot study. Journal of the American College Health Association 27:84–86, 97, 1978

17. Fairburn C: A cognitive behavioral approach to the treatment of bulimia. Psychol Med 11:707–711, 1981

18. Dixon KN, Kiecolt-Glaser J: Group therapy for bulimia. Hillside J Clin Psychiatry (in press)

19. Lacey JH: Bulimia nervosa, binge-eating, and psychogenic vomiting: a controlled treatment study and long term outcome. Br Med J 286:1609–1613, 1983

20. Smith GR: Modification of binge eating in obesity. J Behav Ther Exp Psychiatry 12:333–336, 1981

21. Rosen JC, Leitenberg H: Bulima nervosa: treatment with exposure

and response prevention. Behavior Therapy 13:117–124, 1982

22. Cinciripini PM, Kornblith SJ, Turner SM, et al: A behavioral program for the management of anorexia nervosa and bulimia. J Nerv Ment Dis 171:186–199, 1983

23. Grinc GA: A cognitive-behavioral model for the treatment of chronic vomiting. J Behav Med 5:135–141, 1982

24. Pope HG, Jr, Hudson JI, Jonas JM, et al: Bulimia treated with imipramine: a placebo-controlled, double-blind study. Am J Psychiatry 140:554–558, 1983

25. Wermuth BM, Davis KL, Hollister LE, et al: Phenytoin treatment of the binge-eating syndrome. Am J Psychiatry 134:1249–1253, 1977

26. Hsu LKG: Treatment of bulimia with lithium. Am J Psychiatry 141:1260–1262, 1984

27. Walsh BT, Stewart JW, Roose SP, et al: Treatment of bulimia with phenelzine. Arch Gen Psychiatry 41:1105–1109, 1984

28. Hudson, JI, Pope HG, Jr, Jonas JM, et al: Hypothalamic-pituitary-adrenal axis hyperactivity in bulimia. Psychiatry Res 8:111–117, 1983

7

Treatment of Bulimia With Antidepressants: A Research Update

Harrison G. Pope, Jr., M.D.
James I. Hudson, M.D.
Jeffrey M. Jonas, M.D.
Deborah Yurgelun-Todd, M.S.

7

Treatment of Bulimia With Antidepressants: A Research Update

Previous chapters have reported that a variety of therapeutic methods—including psychodynamic, familial, and group psychotherapy, and several behavioral techniques—have all had some success in the treatment of individual cases of bulimia or in small series of patients. However, none has as yet been shown effective in a *controlled* study in which one group of patients received the therapy in question while a parallel control group simultaneously received a "placebo" treatment. Since bulimia is a spontaneously remitting illness (1, 2) a control group is essential in order to demonstrate that the improvement observed with a given therapy is greater than might be expected by the placebo effect alone.

For some of the therapeutic techniques, even fewer uncontrolled studies are available. To our knowledge, there are no published studies of individual psychodynamic or family therapy in bulimic patients beyond the level of anecdotal case reports. Of three familiar studies of group therapy in bulimia (3–5), two (3, 4) do not provide enough data to allow a determination of efficacy and in addition suffer from serious methodologic limitations (1). The third study (5), although reporting a dramatic decrease in binge-eating behavior among the patients treated, found a marked *increase* in depressive symptoms during treatment—a discouraging result. Although this study was controlled in a sense (one group of patients received group therapy while another waited before beginning the treatment), it was not placebo controlled in the sense that the control subjects received a "treatment" which they thought would help. Instead, the control subjects were aware that they were being required to wait for treatment, and thus presumably had no expectation that they would improve.

In Fairburn's report of behavioral therapy in a group of bulimic patients (6), nine of 11 bulimic patients showed persistent improvement in suppressing binge-eating, lasting for nearly a year. Again, however, the data were uncontrolled, and there is no evidence to document improvement in associated symptoms, such as depression.

ANTIDEPRESSANT THERAPY OF BULIMIA: THEORETICAL RATIONALE

Over the course of the last several years, as previous chapters mentioned, several lines of evidence have suggested that there may be a close relationship between bulimia (and also anorexia nervosa) and major affective disorder—the family of psychiatric disorders which includes major depression and bipolar disorder (manic depressive illness). This evidence falls into four categories.

First, several phenomenologic studies have indicated that patients with bulimia display a very high prevalence of major affective disorder in their personal histories (7, 8). In our center, for example, we have found that approximately 80 percent of bulimic patients have displayed either current or past major depression or bipolar disorder. Furthermore, the depression cannot be explained as merely secondary to binge-eating, since in about 50 percent of patients, the onset of depressive illness occurred a year or more prior to the onset of the bulimic symptoms.

Second, several family studies have indicated that patients with bulimia display a greatly elevated prevalence of major affective disorder in their family trees (9, 10). In fact, we have found in two studies (10, 11) that the prevalence of major depression and bipolar disorder in the first-degree relatives of bulimic patients tends to be slightly (nonsignificantly) higher than that in the first-degree relatives of unipolar depressed patients; the rates more closely resemble those found in the first-degree relatives of bipolar probands. Thus, tentatively, bulimia appears to behave genetically like a "strong" form of affective disorder, a finding congruent with the phenomenological findings discussed above.

Third, several studies of biological tests, including the dexamethasone suppression test (DST) and the thyrotropin-releasing hormone stimulation test (TRH stimulation test), have found a prevalence of abnormal laboratory findings in bulimic patients, comparable to that found in groups of patients with major depression and significantly greater than that found in normal controls or in patients with other psychiatric disorders (12, 13). These results must be interpreted with great caution, however, in that the specificity of both the DST and TRH stimulation tests for major affective disorder remains disputed. If these tests are meaningful, however, the findings further support a link between bulimia and major affective disorder.

Fourth, and of greatest pragmatic value, is the observation that the patients with bulimia respond in a few weeks to antidepressant medications, lithium carbonate, and carbamazepine—medications which are effective in major affective disorder. The first report of a series of bulimic patients treated with antidepressants came from our center (14) in 1982: six of eight patients treated on an open basis with antidepressants experienced a marked decrease in their binge-eating upon treatment. Furthermore, many of these patients had been ill for years prior to the onset of antidepressant therapy; thus, their rapid improvement seems unlikely to represent spontaneous remission. Shortly thereafter a similar report was published by Walsh and colleagues (15). In this study, six patients with bulimia, some of them with chronic and refractory cases, responded with complete or near-complete remission of their bulimic symptoms when treated with monoamine oxidase inhibitors. These findings again suggest a possible relationship between bulimia and major affective disorder, consistent with the findings of the three indices discussed above, and invite more rigorous studies of antidepressant medications in bulimia.

PLACEBO-CONTROLLED, DOUBLE-BLIND STUDIES OF ANTIDEPRESSANTS

To date, five placebo-controlled, double-blind studies of antidepressants have been done with bulimic patients; the results of these studies are summarized below.

In the first study, Sabine et al. used mianserin, a drug not approved for use in the United States, versus placebo in a sample of bulimic patients in Great Britain (16). Neither of the two groups of patients experienced an improvement in their frequency of binge-eating, although both the patients treated with mianserin and those taking placebo improved substantially on most other indices in the study, including ratings of anxiety, depression, eating attitudes, and a "bulimia rating scale."

These results are difficult to interpret. The marked affective improvement in the placebo group does not seem to be attributable to psychotherapy, since contact with all patients was brief. However, some possibility remains that the patients in this study may have been somewhat more suggestible, less severely ill, or in some other way different from the patients described by other investigators. A major question is why neither of the two groups of patients experienced improvement in their frequency of binges. One possible explanation is that the dose of mianserin used in the study was only 60 mg/day, a dose well below that required for an antidepressant effect in some other reports. For example, another recent study (17) found that 150 mg/day was required in many cases. Furthermore, even if it is assumed that the 60 mg/day dose was adequate, it is not clear how much of the drug may have been lost by the study patients as a result of vomiting or laxative abuse. No blood levels of mianserin were provided to document whether adequate amounts were available. Finally, even if the patients were taking and retaining enough mianserin, it may be that mianserin is simply not effective treatment for bulimia. Further studies will be required to differentiate among these various possibilities.

In the second study (18), our group recruited 22 patients with chronic and severe cases of bulimia. These patients binged an average of nine times per week and had been ill an average of seven years. They were assigned to imipramine (11 patients) or placebo (11 patients). Three of the 22 patients dropped out during the six weeks of the study—two because they experienced rashes on imipramine, and one because she became more depressed and took an overdose of her placebo (fortunately with no adverse effects). The latter patient was withdrawn from the study, treated on an open basis with real antidepressants by another physician, and lost to follow-up. Of the remaining 19 patients who completed the study, nine had received imipramine and 10 had received placebo. Of the nine imipramine patients, eight had experienced a "marked" (75–100 percent) or "moderate" (50–75 percent) improvement in their binge-eating. Among the 10 placebo patients, only one had experienced a moderate improvement, eight had experienced no improvement, and one was more than 50 percent worse in terms of binge frequency—a difference significant at the .01 level (Fisher's exact test, two-tailed). In addition, the frequency of binge-eating declined by about 70 percent in the imipramine-treated group but hardly changed at all in the placebo group. Scores on the Hamilton Rating Scale for depression (19) declined 50 percent in the imipramine group and again showed virtually no change in the placebo group. These differences were also significant (both $p < .02$ by Wilcoxon rank sum test, two-tailed).

More important, perhaps, was the finding in this study that patients not only binged less frequently but improved on a number of other measures: they reported significantly less preoccupation with food, less intensity of bingeing, greater self-control with relation to food, and markedly greater subjective global improvement. Furthermore, this improvement persisted on long-term follow-up of up to eight months. We will present two-year follow-up of these patients later in this report.

Three further double-blind studies have now been completed. In the first of these, Walsh and colleagues performed an eight-week placebo-controlled, double-blind study of phenelzine in 25 bulimic patients (20). These patients displayed chronic and refractory cases of bulimia similar to those in the previously described study. The dose of phenelzine used was initially raised to 60 mg/

day, and in some cases raised to 90 mg/day by the sixth week. By the fourth week of phenelzine, significant differences had emerged between the group treated with phenelzine and the group treated with placebo, and these differences were maintained throughout the entire eight weeks of the study. Five of nine phenelzine patients reaching the termination of the study remitted completely, as compared to none of 11 placebo patients. The authors, although impressed with the effects of phenelzine in bulimia, commented on the problems of side effects—notably orthostatic hypertension, which prevented the use of phenelzine at adequate doses in several patients.

In the placebo-controlled, double-blind study performed by Hughes et al. (21), the investigators recruited 22 bulimic patients, comparable in chronicity and severity of illness to those in the two previous studies, and randomized 10 to desipramine and 12 to placebo. Highly significant differences ($p < .01$ or better) emerged between the desipramine-treated patients and the placebo-treated patients on both frequency of binge-eating and several other rating scales. The authors rated nine of the 10 desipramine patients as improved, compared to none of the placebo patients. At the end of the six-week study, the placebo patients were then treated with desipramine on an open basis; 10 of the 12 subsequently improved. Looking at the entire cohort of patients after treatment with desipramine, 12 of the 22 patients were completely free of binge-eating after six weeks and 15 (68 percent) of the 22 patients were free of binge-eating in ten weeks.

Of considerable interest in this study were the Hughes data regarding plasma levels of desipramine. Only six of 20 patients tested for desipramine levels had levels in the range of 125–275 ng/ml. Of the 14 others, 10 had subtherapeutic doses. Six of these 10 had their doses increased to the therapeutic range, and four of these six then became abstinent from binge-eating. This finding emphasizes the need to monitor antidepressant levels in the treatment of bulimic patients in order to optimize response—particularly since some of these patients are likely to lose the drug through purging behavior.

The importance of antidepressant plasma levels is further illustrated in the double-blind study by Mitchell and Groat (22), which compared 16 bulimic subjects treated with amitriptyline to 16 receiving placebo. Plasma levels of amitriptyline were determined for eight of the 16 patients receiving the drug. Of these eight, one had an amitriptyline plus nortriptyline level of zero—raising the possibility that she was not taking her medication at all—and three others had levels below the therapeutic range estimated by most previous studies of amitriptyline plasma levels (23–25). Despite this potentially important limitation, amitriptyline still emerged as significantly superior to placebo on the Hamilton Rating Scale for depression, and also showed a tendency (nonsignificant) to be superior to placebo on all four of the study's measures of eating behavior.

In summary, four of five placebo-controlled, double-blind studies have found marked positive effects for antidepressants in bulimia; the only negative study remains open to methodological questions. It appears reasonable to conclude at this point that tricyclic antidepressants and monoamine oxidase inhibitors (mianserin requires more testing) are frequently and rapidly effective in the treatment of bulimia, and may represent a significant advance in the management of this often serious condition.

Long-term Follow-up

Of course, the effectiveness of antidepressants cannot be considered as established without long-term follow-up data. Does the antidepressant (and antibulimic) effect of the drugs decline as times passes? In order to answer this question, our group did a two-year follow-up on the patients treated in the placebo-controlled, double-blind study described above (26).

Of the 22 patients initially enrolled in our study, 20 were ultimately treated with one or more antidepressant medications. The other two declined treatment (one received placebo and subsequently left the study without trying an antidepressant; the other overdosed on placebo, as described above, and was subsequently treated by an independent psychiatrist and lost to follow-up). Of the remaining 20 patients, two-year follow-up was obtained on 11.

Of these 11, eight (73 percent) were in remission from their bulimia, while the other three displayed, respectively, marked improvement, moderate improvement, and no improvement. Five of the remitted patients remained on antidepressant medication after two years; the other three patients had managed to stop their antidepressants (one after three months, one after seven months, and one after 20 months) and had maintained remission off drug. None of the eight remitted patients received psychotherapy during the follow-up period. The only unimproved patient had formerly shown a moderate response to imipramine and to trazodone but then elected to discontinue antidepressants and continue in psychotherapy; she relapsed to her original level of bingeing and remains at that level at this time.

Of the remaining nine patients in the study, one-year follow-up was obtained on four others (making a total of 15 of 20 patients having received one or more years of follow-up). Of these four patients, two were in remission and two displayed a moderate improvement (50–75 percent decrease in binge-eating) at last follow-up. All were still on medication.

Looking at the status of the entire sample of 20 patients at the time of last follow-up, 10 (50 percent) were in remission, nine (45 percent) were moderately or markedly improved, and only one (5 percent)—who had stopped her medications—was unimproved. These results are summarized in Table 1.

The findings suggest that the quality of improvement experienced on medication does not deteriorate over time. Furthermore, some patients (although to date a minority) have been able to discontinue their medication and remain in remission thereafter.

Table 1. Follow-up of 20 Bulimic Subjects Treated with Antidepressants

	Response			
	None	Moderate	Marked	Remission
Followed more than two years	1	1	1	8
Followed one to two years		2		2
Followed less than one year		3	2	
Total	1 (5%)	6 (30%)	3 (15%)	10 (50%)

CONCLUSION

On the basis of available data, we can draw several conclusions:

1. Antidepressant medications appear to be rapidly effective in a majority of patients with bulimia. Not all patients experience a complete remission of their bulimic symptoms, but at least 80 percent of patients have displayed some response to antidepressants. Furthermore, this response is maintained on long-term follow-up.
2. When using antidepressant medications, it is frequently necessary to try medication from more than one class of antidepressants; patients refractory to tricyclic antidepressants may respond to monoamine oxidase inhibitors, and still other patients may respond to, say, trazodone. In cases where plasma levels are available, it is of critical importance to measure them. Failure to do so may lead to unsatisfactory treatment, well below the potential results available from the drug.
3. Although there are as yet only noncontrolled data to support the efficacy of other therapeutic modalities—such as psychotherapy, behavior therapy, family therapy, or group therapy—in the treatment of bulimia, many bulimic patients, even some of those who have good responses to antidepressants, may benefit from other concomitant therapeutic techniques. Pending adequately controlled data on the efficacy of these techniques, the comments in the last two sections of Chapter Four, by Yager and Edelstein, can guide the clinician as to what type of concomitant nonpharmacologic treatment is indicated for individual cases.

References

1. Pope HG, Jr, Hudson JI: New Hope for Binge Eaters: Advances in the Understanding and Treatment of Bulimia. New York, Harper and Row, 1984

2. Pope HG, Jr, Hudson JI, Yurgelun-Todd D: Anorexia nervosa and bulimia among 300 suburban women shoppers. Am J Psychiatry 141:292–294, 1984

3. Boskind-Lodahl M, White WC: The definition and treatment of bulimarexia in college women: a pilot study. Journal of the American College Health Association 27:84–86, 97, 1978

4. White WC, Boskind-White M: An experiential-behavioral approach to the treatment of bulimarexia. Psychotherapy: Theory, Research, and Practice 8:501–507, 1981

5. Lacey JH: Bulimia nervosa, binge-eating, and psychogenic vomiting: a controlled treatment study and long-term outcome. Br Med J 286:1609–1613, 1983

6. Fairburn CG: A cognitive behavioral approach to the treatment of bulimia. Psychol Med 11:707–711, 1981

7. Hudson JI, Pope HG, Jr, Jonas JM, et al: Phenomenologic relationship of eating disorders to major affective disorder. Psychiatry Res 9:345–354, 1983

8. Walsh BT, Roose SP, Glassman AH, et al: Bulimia and depression. Psychosomat Med 47:123–131, 1985

9. Pyle RL, Mitchell JE, Eckert ED: Bulimia: a report of 34 cases. J Clin Psychiatry 42:60–64, 1981

10. Hudson JI, Pope HG, Jr, Jonas JM, et al: Family history study of anorexia nervosa and bulimia. Br J Psychiatry 142:133–138, 1983

11. Pope HG, Jr, Hudson JI, Jonas JM, et al: Controlled family history study of active and remitted bulimic subjects. Paper presented at the

First International Conference on Eating Disorders. New York, April 1984

12. Hudson JI, Pope HG, Jr, Jonas JM, et al: Hypothalamic-pituitary-adrenal axis hyperactivity in bulimia. Psychiatry Res 8:111–117, 1983

13. Roy-Byrne P, Gwirtsman H, Yager J, et al: Neuroendocrine abnormalities in bulimia. Am J Psychiatry 140:559–563, 1983

14. Pope HG, Jr, Hudson JI: Treatment of bulimia with antidepressants. Psychopharmacology 78:167–179, 1982

15. Walsh BT, Stewart JW, Wright L, et al: Treatment of bulimia with monoamine oxidase inhibitors. Am J Psychiatry 139:1629–1630, 1982

16. Sabine EJ, Yonace A, Farrington AJ, et al: Bulimia nervosa: a placebo-controlled double-blind therapeutic trial of mianserin. Br J Clin Pharmacol 15:195S–202S, 1983

17. McGrath PJ, Quitkin FM, Stewart JW, et al: An open clinical trail of mianserin. Am J Psychiatry 138:530–532, 1981

18. Pope HG, Jr, Hudson JI, Jonas JM, et al: Bulimia treated with imipramine: a placebo-controlled, double-blind study. Am J Psychiatry 140:554–558, 1983

19. Hamilton M: A rating scale for depression. J Neurol Neurosurg Psychiatry 23:56–62, 1960

20. Walsh BT, Stewart JW, Roose SP, et al: Treatment of bulimia with phenelzine: a double-blind, placebo-controlled study. Arch Gen Psychiatry 41:1105–1109, 1984

21. Hughes PL, Wells LA, Cunningham CJ, et al: Treating bulimia with desipramine: a placebo-controlled double-blind study. Arch Gen Psychiatry, in press

22. Mitchell JE, Groat R: A placebo-controlled double-blind trial of amitryptyline in bulimia. J Clin Psychopharmacol 4:186–193, 1984

23. Braithwaite RA, Goulding R, Theano G, et al: Plasma concentration of amitriptyline and clinical response. Lancet 1:1297, 1972

24. Zeigler VE, Clayton PJ, Biggs JT: A comparison study of amitriptyline and nortriptyline with plasma levels. Arch Gen Psychiatry 34:607–612, 1977

25. Kupfer DJ, Hanin I, Spiker DG, et al: Amitriptyline plasma levels and clinical response in primary depression. Clin Pharmacol Ther 22:904–911, 1977

26. Pope HG, Jr, Jonas JM, et al: Antidepressant treatment of bulimia: a two-year follow-up study. J Clin Psychopharmacol, in press